Juices & Smoothies

Juices & Smoothies

OVER 160 HEALTHY,
REFRESHING AND
IRRESISTIBLE
DRINKS AND BLENDS

SUZANNAH OLIVIER

WITH RECIPES BY
JOANNA FARROW

JG
PRESS

Published by World Publications Group, Inc.

140 Laurel Street, East Bridgewater, MA 02333

www.wrldpub.net

Produced by Anness Publishing Ltd

Hermes House, 88–89 Blackfriars Road, London SE1 8HA

tel. 020 7401 2077; fax 020 7633 9499

www.annesspublishing.com

If you like the images in this book and would like to investigate using them for publishing, promotions or advertising, please visit our website www.practicalpictures.com for more information.

Publisher: Joanna Lorenz

Managing Editor: Linda Fraser

Editor: Clare Gooden

Production Controller: Wendy Lawson

Designer: Nigel Partridge

Photography by Gus Filgate and Craig Robertson, with additional pictures by
Janine Hosegood and Simon Smith

Stylist: Helen Trent

Additional recipes by Susannah Blake, Nicola Graimes and Jane Milton

ETHICAL TRADING POLICY

Because of our ongoing ecological investment programme, you, as our customer, can have the pleasure and reassurance of knowing that a tree is being cultivated on your behalf to naturally replace the materials used to make the book you are holding. For further information about this scheme, go to www.annesspublishing.com/trees

ISBN-10: 1-57215-494-2

ISBN-13: 978-1-57215-494-0

Printed and Bound in China

NOTES

Bracketed terms are intended for American readers.

For all recipes, quantities are given in both metric and imperial measures and, where appropriate, measures are also given in standard cups and spoons. Follow one set, but not a mixture, because they are not interchangeable.

Standard spoon and cup measures are level. 1 tsp = 5ml, 1 tbsp = 15ml, 1 cup = 250ml/8fl oz

Australian standard tablespoons are 20ml. Australian readers should use 3 tsp in place of 1 tbsp for measuring small quantities of gelatine, flour, salt, etc.

American pints are 16fl oz/2 cups. American readers should use 20fl oz/2.5 cups in place of 1 pint when measuring liquids.

Electric oven temperatures in this book are for conventional ovens. When using a fan oven, the temperature will probably need to be reduced by about 10–20°C/20–40°F. Since ovens vary, you should check with your manufacturer's instruction book for guidance.

Medium (US large) eggs are used unless otherwise stated.

The very young, elderly and those in ill-health or with a compromised immune system are advised against consuming juices or blends that contain raw eggs.

Always check the manufacturer's instructions before using a blender or food processor to crush ice.

CONTENTS

Introduction

Juices, smoothies, shakes and blends have become extremely popular in recent years. They fit neatly into hectic modern lives, enabling you to incorporate healthy habits into your everyday routines. The main advantage of juices and smoothies is that they are easy to make, quick, convenient and packed with rejuvenating, healing and revitalizing nutrients. On top of all this, they are also delicious, and a luxurious blended drink can feel like a real treat.

The Benefits of Juicing

While you can buy ready-made juices and smoothies, nothing quite beats the taste of a blend made at home. Freshly made juices are also a more potent source of nutrients and certain combinations have specific health benefits. If you drink juices or blends on a regular basis, you'll enjoy clearer skin, better energy levels and balanced overall health. It is also well known that the antioxidants found in fruits and vegetables work most effectively when they are consumed together, and juicing encourages precisely this.

Above: Fresh flavours are whizzed up into nutrient-packed blends in minutes.

Combinations of specific different juices can be used to emphasize particular flavours or effects in the same way that you would in cooking – sweet and sour, savoury and spicy, warming or cooling – but you can afford to be more adventurous than you might be with conventionally prepared foods. The juice of a fruit or vegetable often tastes much better than when the produce is cooked or even served raw. For instance, you may not particularly like celery as a vegetable, but juice it and combine the juice with pear and ginger and you get a completely different, more complex and utterly delicious taste sensation.

Even if you feel like going off the rails and indulging in extra ingredients, such as chocolate, alcohol or coffee, the very fact that the juice or smoothie is based on fresh fruits and vegetables means that you are still getting a wonderful boost of vitamins, antioxidants and minerals – healthy in anyone's book.

Preparing juices and blends also has a psychological benefit. The very act of making a juice or smoothie can make you feel good – you will feel you are nurturing and pampering yourself – and

Left: Let children get involved in juicing and watch them reap the benefits.

in addition, by using lots of fresh natural ingredients you will boost your own health and the health of your family. Juices and smoothies are great fun to make and to share: encourage your children to invent concoctions and join in the preparation, or share a juice instead of coffee with a friend.

The History of Juicing and Blending

As long ago as the 19th century, doctors and naturopaths were using fresh fruit and vegetable juices to improve the health of their patients. Many well-known pioneers were responsible for researching and creating the wealth of knowledge and evidence we now have about the therapeutic properties of juices. People such as Dr Kellogg, Father Kniepp, Dr Max Bircher-Bener and Dr Max Gerson all helped to popularize the notion of the "juice cure".

However, there is evidence to suggest that juicing is even older than this in the ancient practices of wine

Below: The process of making juices is as enjoyable as drinking them.

and scrumpy (apple cider) making. After extracting the fresh fruit juices, fermenting them into alcohol was simply a way of preserving the raw ingredients – and in those days drinking alcohol was safer than drinking water, which was often contaminated. The healing power of certain foods was even recognized by Hippocrates who said "Let food be your medicine." Indeed, since time immemorial, food, water and healing herbs have been the cornerstones of the healing arts.

The modern concept of blending drinks and making smoothies probably began with mixed drinks such as cocktails. For the more virtuous and health-conscious among us, however, non-alcoholic juices and blends have always sat comfortably alongside the bar choice.

We are going through a change in how we involve ourselves in our health. Reliance on prepared and fast foods has given way to a re-emergence of interest in healthy eating messages – the most familiar of these is that we need to eat five portions of fruit and vegetables every day. One convenient way of achieving this, in the context of

Above: Raw ingredients that can be juiced provide all the vitamins and minerals that you need to stay healthy.

our modern, fast-paced lives, is to embrace health drinks as easy-to-make snacks, quick breakfasts and fast energy boosters. The introduction of advanced kitchen technology, such as blenders, food processors and juicers, has made the preparation of blends and juices quick and easy.

In recent years, we have become more and more interested in natural ways of improving our health – echoing the thoughts and practices of the pioneering enthusiasts of earlier centuries. In addition to their more general health-boosting properties, juices and blends are also used for specific cleansing and detoxing, for helping speed recovery from illness and as part of anti-ageing regimes. There is also a school of thought that maintains that juices can help prevent some cancers, although this has yet to be proven. Nevertheless, freshly made fruit and vegetable juices provide many of the essential vitamins and minerals that are vital for a healthy life.

It is not often that something so healthy also tastes so good and is a pleasure to incorporate into daily life. Perhaps this is why juices, blended drinks, smoothies and shakes are standing the test of time.

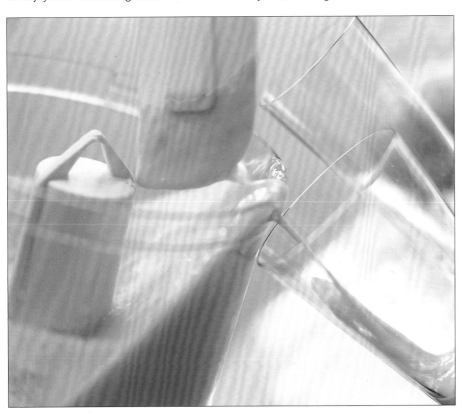

the art of juicing and blending

Learn about juicing and blending techniques.
Discover the best equipment to use for each drink,
which ingredients work well together and how to get
the most nutrients from your blend.

Getting equipped

For successful juicing and blending, you will need some basic equipment. The chances are that you will have several items, such as a citrus press or a blender, already, but there are some more specialist items available that will make the job easier, quicker and much more fun.

Centrifugal Juicers

These come in a variety of designs. They are the least expensive type of electric juicer, yet are perfectly adequate for most juices. They have a pulp collector into which the fibre and pulp residue is ejected. Some come with a jug (pitcher) attachment that collects the juice; others require a separate jug or glass to be placed under the spout. Centrifugal juicers work by finely grating vegetables and fruit, and spinning them at great speed, which separates the juice from the pulp. Juicers are used to extract juice from hard vegetables and fruit, such as carrots and apples, and from leafy vegetables.

BUYING TIPS

When deciding what equipment to buy, think about what you want to make. Do you prefer smoothies or is vegetable juicing a priority? Juicers are best for firm vegetables and fruit, such as carrot, apples and green leaves, but they are not good for soft fruit, such as bananas and mangoes, which clog up the machine and do not provide much juice. On the other hand, blenders are ideal for soft fruit and allow you to retain all the fibre. Before buying, ask yourself the following questions.

• Is it easy to feed the fruit and vegetables into the machine?
• If you are going to make large quantities, does the machine allow you to do this? How much pulp residue is collected?
• Are there any awkward corners to get into when cleaning? Round containers are usually easier to clean.
• Is the machine easy to assemble and take apart?
• Are any parts easily breakable? Make sure that removable parts are easy to replace if necessary.
• Is a jug (pitcher) provided or will you need to get hold of a container to collect the juice?
• Does the machine have a see-through container or lid so you can see what is happening inside?
• Is the power of the motor suitable? Some models have two-speed motors; others just have one speed. Decide which you need.
• Do you need to be able to crush ice? If so, check that the machine is suitable for this purpose.

Above: Centrifugal juicers are quick, easy to use and relatively cheap.

Masticating Juicers

These are more high-tech than centrifugal juicers, and also more expensive. Instead of shredding the produce they finely chop it and then force the pulp through a mesh to separate out the juice. Electric or manually operated, masticating juicers produce a greater volume of juice than centrifugal models and, because of the method of extraction, the juice contains more live enzymes. In addition to using masticating juicers to make juices you could also use them to make delicious nut butters, ice cream from frozen fruit ingredients and healthy baby foods. Some masticating juicers come with useful attachments for milling grains, otherwise you can buy the attachments separately.

Food Processors

These multi-functional machines comprise a main bowl and a variety of attachments, some of which are supplied with the original purchase; others can be bought individually. For making juices and blends, the most important attachments are:

• A strong blade that blends medium-hard or soft fruit and vegetables.

• A centrifugal juicing attachment that turns your food processor into a juicer. This is not as efficient as a dedicated juicer, but is a good option if you juice only occasionally or have limited storage space.

• A citrus press attachment.

• Whisking attachments.

• Ice crushing attachments.

Blenders

These feature a plastic or glass jug (pitcher) placed on top of a motorized base, which powers blades inside the jug. Blenders work best with soft fruit, such as bananas, peaches and berries, to which you add a liquid ingredient, such as water, milk or juice, to create delicious smoothies and shakes. Some can also be used to crush ice, but always check the instructions.

Above: Your food processor needs a strong blade for blending harder fruits.

Below: Blenders turn soft fruits into delicious smoothies and milkshakes.

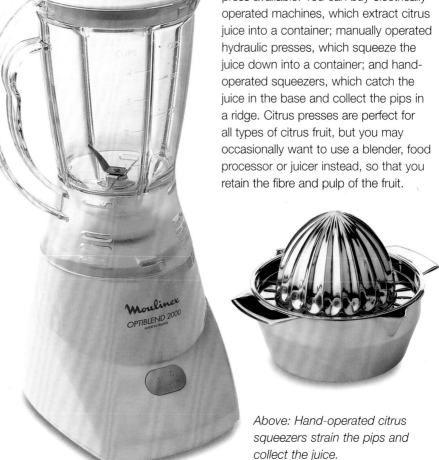

THE FIBRE ISSUE

Smoothies made in a blender are different from juices made in a juicer in one important way: they retain the fibre of the fruits. Fibre is not only important for healthy digestion, but also for cardiovascular health, and for helping balance blood-sugar levels. When choosing equipment, bear in mind that fibre is valuable in the diet and, while juicing will not replace eating whole fruits and vegetables, smoothies and other blended drinks are nutritionally equivalent to eating the whole fruit. However, nutritional guidelines state that one glass of juice does count towards the recommended total daily intake of five portions of fruit and vegetables.

Citrus Juicers

There are three main types of citrus press available. You can buy electrically operated machines, which extract citrus juice into a container; manually operated hydraulic presses, which squeeze the juice down into a container; and hand-operated squeezers, which catch the juice in the base and collect the pips in a ridge. Citrus presses are perfect for all types of citrus fruit, but you may occasionally want to use a blender, food processor or juicer instead, so that you retain the fibre and pulp of the fruit.

Above: Hand-operated citrus squeezers strain the pips and collect the juice.

Vegetable scrubbing brush Use a firm brush to remove dirt from your vegetables, particularly root vegetables, as an alternative to peeling.

Zester A zester is extremely useful for grating rind and adding intense citrus flavour to juices and blends. The row of holes at the top of the zester shaves off thin shreds of rind, leaving the bitter white pith behind.

Canelle knife This tool has a tooth-like blade that pares off the rind in ribbons or julienne strips. Combined zester/canelle knives are also available.

Below: Citrus zesters and canelle knives are useful for preparing fruit.

Electric Wand

These handheld electric mixers are good for no-fuss blending. Some models come with a variety of attachments for blending and whisking. You need to use an electric wand with a deep bowl, or a flask (which is sometimes supplied). If you are going to blend on a regular basis it is much more practical to buy a proper blender, although handheld wands can blend soft fruit and liquid, syrup or powdered ingredients well. Creamy whipped toppings can be made with the whisk attachment.

Below: Always use a good sharp knife to peel and chop fruit and vegetables.

Above: Handheld blender wands are easy to use and very effective.

Other Useful Equipment

Chopping board Buy a big chopping board that will accommodate large quantities of fruits and vegetables. Plastic boards are easier to keep clean than wooden ones. To clean chopping boards, scrub with washing-up liquid (dishwashing detergent), then allow them to air dry – drying with a cloth often leads to recontamination. To avoid contamination, use a separate chopping board for raw fruit, vegetables and bread, and keep another for meat.

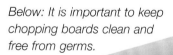

Below: It is important to keep chopping boards clean and free from germs.

Apple corer These make quick work of coring apples or pears before you blend them. Place over the core at the stem end and push down firmly right through the fruit, then twist slightly and pull out the core and pips. There is no need to core apples or pears if you are putting them through a juicer.

Sharp knife Make sure your knife is really sharp because this will make chopping much easier, and safer too.

Plastic spatula These are handy for scraping thick blends out of a blender or food processor, and the plastic will not scratch the equipment.

Above: Ice cream scoops are available in many different shapes and styles.

Above: Sieves can be used to strain thick blends or to remove large seeds.

Above: For exact amounts, use a set of measuring jugs and spoons.

Cherry stoner This simple tool takes the hard work out of pitting cherries and makes it much quicker. The bowl of the implement has a hole through which the cherry stone is ejected when the fruit is pressed.

Melon baller Insert this small round scoop into the melon flesh and twist to remove neat balls of fruit.

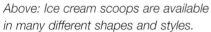

*Above:
A cherry stoner,
an apple corer
and a melon baller*

Measuring jugs Available in either glass or plastic and in many different sizes, measuring jugs (pitchers) must have the measurements clearly marked for ease of use. It's worth buying a large measuring jug.

Sieve This can be useful when you want to strain juices to remove seeds and pips for fussy children, or if you just want a thinner juice.

Vegetable peeler For preparing some root vegetables, such as potatoes and carrots, you will need a sturdy vegetable peeler. There are two main types available: straight blade or swivel blade. Experiment with each before choosing the one you feel most comfortable with, as this can make the job much easier.

Ice cream scoops These are useful for scooping ice cream, frozen yogurt or sorbet into milkshakes or smoothies. Choose from half-moon-shaped stainless-steel scoops with sleek steel handles, simple spoon-shaped scoops with metal handles or easy-grip moulded plastic handles, or brightly coloured plastic scoops with quick release levers. For smaller rounds of sorbet or frozen yogurt, try using a melon baller as a scoop.

Above: There are many different types of vegetable peeler.

Storage jug or vacuum flask Choose a storage jug (pitcher) with a close-fitting lid or place clear film (plastic wrap) over the opening before securing the lid. Covering the juice or blend securely limits its exposure to oxygen and prevents it from oxidizing. Even better, use a wide-necked vacuum flask.

Serving jugs and glasses Buy different shapes and colours and have some fun with these, contrasting them with the colour of the juice or smoothie you are serving.

Juicing and blending techniques

Once you have purchased the necessary equipment for juicing or blending you will want to get started as soon as possible. For maximum freshness and flavour, prepare the fruit and vegetables just before you are ready to juice them. There are slightly different requirements for preparing produce for each type of machine. Always read the equipment manufacturer's instructions first.

Centrifugal and Masticating Juicers

Although centrifugal and masticating juicers function in different ways, the preparation of fruits and vegetables, and the basic principles for using the machines, are much the same.

1 Always choose firm produce as soft fruits will not give successful results. For instance, firm, underripe pears work well, but soft, ripe pears are best prepared in a blender or food processor.

2 Prepare the produce. Most fruit and vegetables do not need to be cored or peeled – although you might prefer to core fruit – as peel, pips (seeds) and core will simply be turned into pulp in the machine.

3 Scrub any produce you are not going to peel with a hard brush under cold running water to get rid of any dirt. If there is a waxy residue, then use a little bit of soap or washing-up liquid (dishwashing detergent) to help dissolve this, then rinse the produce thoroughly under cold running water.

4 Large stones (pits) of fruit such as peaches and plums need to be removed. Cut round the middle of the fruit, using a small, sharp knife, then twist to break into two halves. Carefully ease out the stone with the knife. Mangoes have a large, flat stone. Peel the fruit, then cut the flesh away from either side of the stone, then remove as much flesh as possible from the stone.

5 All leafy vegetables, such as cabbages and lettuces, can be put through a juicer. Include the outer leaves, which are nutritionally superior, although these must be washed thoroughly first.

6 Citrus fruit can be put through a juicer. Ensure that you remove all the peel, but there is no need to remove the pips or pith.

7 When pushing the produce through the feeder tube of the machine, it is very important that you use the plunger provided. Remember to position a jug (pitcher) or glass under the nozzle of the machine to catch the juice, otherwise it will spray all over the work surface.

8 Put the ingredients through the machine in manageable quantities. Cut pears and apples into quarters, for example, and alternate them if possible to ensure that the juices mix well. If you push too many pieces of fruit or vegetable through in one go, or push through pieces that are too large, the machine will clog up.

9 Push through a hard ingredient, such as a carrot, after softer ingredients, such as cabbage. This will keep the juice flowing freely and will prevent blockages.

Cleaning Juicers, Blenders and Food Processors

The one and only dreary thing about making delicious juices and blends is that the equipment needs to be cleaned soon afterwards. However, there are some simple, no-fuss ways of making this chore much easier.

Cleaning a juicer, blender or food processor thoroughly is important if you want to avoid unwanted and unhealthy bacteria, and the best time to do this is straight after you have made the juice or smoothie and poured it into glasses or a jug (pitcher). If you clean the parts of a juicer, blender or food processor immediately (or at least put them in to soak), the pulp and residue should just rinse off easily.

1 To clean a centrifugal or masticating juicer, blender or food processor, fill a sink with cold water and carefully take the equipment apart, following the manufacturer's instructions.

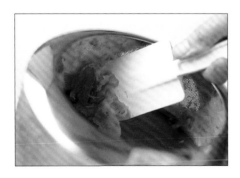

2 Using a plastic spatula or spoon, scoop off any large pieces of residue (such as the fruit and vegetable pulp that collects inside the spout of the juicer or around the blades) and discard it. Better still, if you have a compost heap in the garden, add the fruit or vegetable residue to it.

3 Plunge the non-electrical, removable machine parts of the juicer, blender or food processor into the sink full of cold water and leave them to soak until you are ready to clean them – this will probably be after you've sat back and enjoyed your freshly made juice or blend. Soaking the machine parts will help to loosen any remaining fruit and vegetable pulp and will make cleaning them much easier.

4 After soaking, either carefully handwash the non-electrical, removable machine parts or put them into a dishwasher on a normal setting.

5 Scrub any attachments that you have used with a firm brush to loosen any residue that remains. Take care when handling grating attachments as they are extremely sharp.

6 The removable components of your juicer, blender or food processor may occasionally get stained, especially if you regularly make juices with vibrantly coloured ingredients such as blackberries or beetroot. Soak these stained components every now and then in plenty of cold water with a little bleach added. Be sure to rinse the parts thoroughly afterwards, then leave them until they are completely dry before putting the machine back together.

TROUBLESHOOTING

If you experience any problems using your juicer, or if the resulting drink is not quite what you imagined, the following may help.

The machine gets clogged up
Push a hard fruit or vegetable, such as carrot or apple, through the machine to keep the juice flowing.

The taste of one ingredient is overwhelming the juice
Increase the quantity of another ingredient, use a base juice to dilute the flavours or add a splash of lemon or lime juice to help rescue the juice.

The blend is too thin
Add an ingredient to thicken the drink, such as yogurt, cream, banana or avocado.

TROUBLESHOOTING

If you experience any problems using a blender or food processor, or if the resulting drink is not quite what you imagined, the following may help.

The blend is too thick

Thin it using water or the juice of a watery fruit. For a pure taste, use fruit juice to dilute a fruit purée made in a blender.

The blend is too pulpy

Strain the mixture through a sieve, pressing the pulp down with the back of a spoon.

The ingredients get stuck to the side of the bowl

Scrape down the mixture with a plastic spatula to ensure that all ingredients are mixed thoroughly.

Blenders and Food Processors

These machines work in fairly similar ways, and the preparation of fruit is the same for both types of equipment. The main difference is the point at which you add liquid. Blenders and food processors are best used for soft fruits.

1 Fruits with inedible skins, such as bananas, mangoes and papayas, should be peeled.

2 Fruits with edible skins, such as peaches or plums, do not need to be peeled but should be washed thoroughly. If you prefer a juice with a finer, smoother texture, peel the fruits before blending.

3 Fruits with large stones (pits), cores or pips (seeds), such as mangoes, plums, cherries and apples, should be stoned (pitted), cored or seeded.

4 Fruits with tiny seeds, such as raspberries, strawberries or kiwis, can be used whole, when the seeds add texture and a pretty speckled effect. However, if you prefer a smooth drink, the pulp can be pushed through a fine sieve, using a plastic spatula, to remove the seeds.

5 When using berries and currants, remove the stalks and leaves and wash the fruit thoroughly. An easy way to detach, or string, redcurrants, blackcurrants or whitecurrants from their stalks is to hold the bunch firmly at the top, then slowly draw the tines of a fork through the fruit so that the currants fall away.

6 To blend fruit in a food processor, place it in the bowl of the machine and process to a thick pulp. Add any liquid or creamy ingredient, such as water, fruit juice, milk or yogurt, and process again.

7 To blend fruit in a blender, it is important to add the liquid ingredients and the soft fruit at the same time, then process altogether, otherwise the blades will not be able to blend the fruits effectively.

8 If using a handheld electric wand, remember that this piece of equipment is not as powerful as other juicers or blenders. Use only very soft fruits, such as bananas, peaches and berries, as it cannot cope with anything firmer.

Citrus Juicers

1 First, cut the citrus fruit in half using a sharp knife.

2 To use a traditional handheld juicer, press the cut half over the cone of the juicer and, using an even pressure all round, twist the fruit to squeeze out as much juice as possible. The rim of the squeezer will catch any pips (seeds) but you may need a bowl to catch the juice.

3 To use a juicer with a citrus attachment or an electrically operated citrus juicer, firmly press the halved fruit over the spinning cone of the juicer. The motor will turn the cone under the fruit, and this will extract more juice than a handheld juicer would usually produce.

4 To use a manual hydraulic press, place a container under the juice nozzle to collect the juice (unless one is supplied as part of the juicer) and place the halved citrus fruit in the press. Pull the lever forwards to apply pressure and squeeze out the juice.

5 To use a centrifugal or masticating juicer, remove the citrus peel with a sharp knife (there is no need to worry about removing the pips or the white pith that remains). Cut the fruit into similar-sized chunks or break into segments, then press the fruit through the juicer funnel.

QUICK START TIPS

If you are impatient to get going, you can achieve some delicious instant results with one of these simple basic blends.

Banana and Berry Milkshake
1 banana
generous handful of strawberries, raspberries or other soft berries
1 glass cold milk or soya milk

Peel the banana and chop into chunks. Put all the ingredients in a blender or food processor. Blend, pour into a glass and serve.

Carrot and Apple Juice
2 large carrots
1 apple

Wash the carrots and apple, cut into chunks and push through a juicer. Spoon off any foam, if you prefer, and serve.

Lemon and Orange Refresher
1 orange
½ lemon
sparkling water
5ml/1 tsp sugar (optional)
ice cubes and/or fresh mint leaves

Juice the fruit in a juicer. Add the sparkling water and sugar, if using. Pour into a glass, add ice cubes and/or mint leaves, then serve.

Tomato and Pepper Boost
½ red (bell) pepper
150g/5oz tomatoes
juice of ½ lime
ice cubes

Soak the tomatoes in boiling water, then peel off the skin and chop into chunks. Halve the red pepper, remove the seeds and chop into similar-sized chunks. Add the pepper and tomatoes to a blender or food processor and blend well. Add a squeeze of lime juice and some ice cubes, then serve.

Serving and storing juices, smoothies and blends

The ideal way to enjoy juices, blends and smoothies is to drink them immediately. This way you benefit from the full flavour and nutritional benefits, because time and exposure to oxygen take their toll on the nutrient content of most prepared fruits and vegetables. For instance, when you make carrot juice, it is a bright orange colour, but if you leave it for an hour it will turn brown as it oxidizes. Likewise, the flesh of apples or avocados turns brown as it oxidizes and loses nutritional value.

Serving and Decorating Juices and Drinks

There are many attractive and quirky ways to serve fresh drinks. With a little forethought and imagination, you can present friends and family with gorgeous-looking concoctions – whatever the occasion.

Adding ice Ice is a wonderful vehicle for serving, cooling and decorating drinks. Cubes are best for cooling drinks, and these can be decorated or flavoured in different ways. A handful of ice can be added to a drink, or you can add crushed ice to drinks in glasses to cool them quickly.

Fruit ice cubes Place raspberries or other small fruits in an ice-cube tray and add water.

Flower and petal ice cubes Choose flowers that will be attractive even when the ice has melted – rose petals, carnation pinks or borage flowers.

Sugar-rimmed glasses Moisten the rim of a glass with water, dip into grated lemon or lime rind and then into icing (confectioners') sugar.

Fruit purée drizzle For a striped effect, pour fruit purée down the inside of glasses before adding the drink.

Juicy ice cubes Make cubes from orange, cranberry or diluted lime juice in an ice-cube tray. Thse will create a rainbow effect in your drinks and will also alter the taste as they melt.

Right: Suspend sprigs of currants over your drinks for a stunning effect.

Edible swizzle sticks These can be fun and celery sticks are a natural choice for savoury drinks. Finely slice one end of the stick then soak in iced water for about 15 minutes – a fanned out fringe will develop.

Fruit skewers Place fruit segments or currants on a skewer and use as a swizzle stick. Bruised lemon grass stalks, lavender or rosemary stems, or cinnamon sticks can also be used.

Glass decorations Place fruit slices on the rim of a glass or skewer small pieces of fruit on to cocktail sticks (toothpicks) and balance these across the tops of glasses. Experiment with herb leaves and pared citrus rind.

Ice lollies Fruit juices make healthy ice lollies (popsicles) for children. All you need is an inexpensive mould, available from kitchenware shops. This is a fun way to serve drinks at parties.

Storage of Juices and Drinks

While it is definitely best to serve juices and smoothies when they are just freshly made, you may want to store them for one reason or another. Perhaps you have made too much to drink in one go, maybe you have a glut of berries or some other produce that you need to use up before it over-ripens, or you might simply want to take a juice or smoothie into work for a healthy mid-morning snack.

One way to minimize the oxidization of juices is to add some vitamin C. Either squeeze in a little fresh lemon or orange juice or add 2.5ml/½ tsp of powdered vitamin C, which is available from health food shops. Juices can then be stored in the refrigerator for a few hours and won't discolour – make sure you chill them as soon as possible after making.

Above: To make children's parties fun, try serving fresh juices frozen into lollies.

To store a juice or smoothie pour it into a jar or jug (pitcher), filling it right to the brim. Seal with clear film (plastic wrap) or, alternatively, use a screw-top jug or vacuum flask.

Most juices can be frozen for use at a later date and this will preserve almost all of their full nutritional value. Try freezing different flavoured juices in ice-cube trays – the ice cubes can then simply be removed and added to drinks. Otherwise, try to freeze the juice in fairly small amounts (glassfuls). Any juice or blended drink can be frozen successfully, but it is a good idea to make single ingredient base juices to freeze, because you can then add different flavourings when the juice is thawed. Make sure you label and date the containers clearly.

Buying produce

If you are really enthusiastic about making juices, blends and smoothies you may want to bulk buy some of the basic ingredients. Carrots, apples, bananas, pineapples and oranges are often used as base juices to which other ingredients are added. Additional ingredients, such as summer berries, are best used when really fresh and so should be juiced on the day of purchase.

Freshness

The produce you use for juices, smoothies and blends should be as fresh as possible to ensure that you will get the maximum nutrients from your drinks. It is not necessary to buy produce that looks perfect, but do avoid any that is bruised, damaged or overripe. Aim to buy fruit and vegetables that are in season if you can. By buying seasonally and locally, your produce will be bursting with health-boosting vitamins and minerals.

Ripeness

The riper the fruit, the more sugar it will contain and the sweeter it will be. It also means that the fruit contains more nutrients, especially if the produce has been ripened on the tree or plant. Fruits that are picked green and ripened in transit contain fewer nutrients.

Storage

All fruit and vegetables benefit from being stored in cool, dry conditions. However, if fruit is slightly underripe and too firm to be juiced, find a sunny windowsill on which to ripen it for a couple of days. Avoid wrapping produce in plastic bags as it cannot breathe. Ideally you should store ingredients in individual bowls or trays – for instance, one for citrus fruits, one for bananas and one for onions – as they all have different ripening times and one item can affect another, leading to premature rotting.

Above: Buy produce that is ripe if you can, but if it is needs further ripening, simply leave it on a sunny windowsill.

Organic Produce

Food that is grown organically is slightly more expensive than regular produce, but there are some clear advantages in choosing it.

The levels of chemicals that you are exposed to via pesticides, fungicides and fertilizers will be significantly reduced if you choose organic produce. Advocates of organic fruit and vegetables also claim that they taste better because there is less water bulking out the produce. It is certainly true that if you taste an organic carrot and then compare it to the taste of a non-organic carrot, the former will usually have a more solid texture and a stronger, more intense carroty taste. This inevitably means that your blends will have more flavour, as there will be less water diluting the juice.

Even if you don't want to buy entirely organic produce, you may want to consider buying bulky base items, such as carrots and apples, from organic ranges.

Left: Organic fruits tend to contain less water so the taste is more intense, and they are exposed to fewer pesticides.

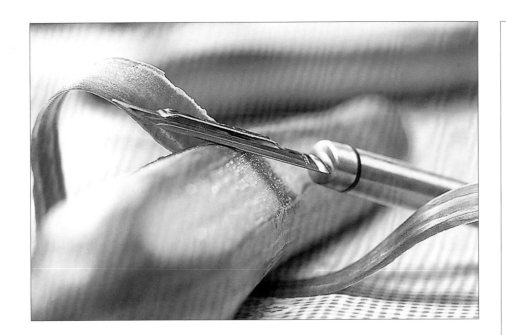

Above: It may be worth peeling the skin of non-organic produce, as this will remove any possible chemical residue.

Convenient Options

For convenience, and because you can't always find fresh produce out of season, it is worthwhile keeping some dried, frozen, canned and bottled fruits or vegetables to hand in your store cupboard (pantry). Use these as substitutes whenever you run out of a fresh ingredient or if you find that an ingredient is unavailable or out of season. Choose fruits that are preserved in unsweetened fruit juice in preference to syrup, as this is a more natural state. Dried fruit is also a useful standby, especially dried apricots, dates and figs.

Frozen fruit such as strawberries, raspberries, blueberries and bags of frozen mixed summer fruits work very well in smoothies and blended drinks. If blended straight from the freezer, they turn smoothies into deliciously chilled slushes and you will not need to add any additional ice.

Whole nuts and seeds (for grinding into blends or for sprinkling on top of drinks as decoration) and dry ingredients such as wheatgerm should be kept in airtight jars or packets and stored in the refrigerator to keep them fresh once opened. However, because of their high fat content, nuts and seeds will become rancid if you keep them for too long. Make sure you buy from a supplier with a rapid turnover and always check the use-by date on the packet before you add them to drinks.

IRRADIATION
Most herbs and spices are irradiated (treated with radiation to delay spoiling) but this is forbidden with organic produce. If you wish to avoid irradiated herbs and spices you need to buy organic.

GM CROPS
Genetically modified foods are a recent innovation. If you have concerns about this type of produce, buy organic fruit and vegetables. Be aware that most soya products are GM-based, so look in your local health food shop and choose products that state they contain "non-genetically modified soya" on the packet.

Below: To avoid genetically modified produce, buy organic – it is worth spending a little bit more.

Citrus fruit

To juice citrus fruits you will need to use a citrus juicer, and the juice can then be added to other blends if desired. Oranges are available all year round and store well in cool, dry conditions. All citrus fruits are rich in vitamin C, and one large orange provides your recommended daily allowance (RDA). Oranges, tangerines, mandarins and other citrus fruits are also excellent sources of folic acid. As an alternative to using a citrus juicer, you could push the peeled fruit through a juicer to benefit from the fibre and pith. The pith is rich in two bioflavonoids, rutin and hesperidin, which aid the absorption of vitamin C and strengthen blood vessels. The rind is rich in limonene, which is very good for liver health. However, some people find that certain citrus fruits are too acidic for their digestive system.

Preparing and Juicing Citrus Fruits

To juice citrus fruits, you will need a citrus juicer (handheld, electric or hydraulic), a chopping board and a sharp knife. If you are going to use the rind, you will also need a scrubbing brush, soap or washing-up liquid (dishwashing detergent), and a grater.

Juicing The simplest way to juice citrus fruits is to cut them in half and squeeze out the juice using a handheld juicer or a reamer. A hydraulic citrus press or citrus attachment on a citrus juicer is more efficient, however, and will produce more juice. Press the cut fruit against the cone of the juicer. Peeled fruits can also be juiced in a juicer or blended using a food processor or blender.

Grating rind If you wish to use rind in a juice, choose a non-waxed organic fruit to avoid chemical residue or scrub the skin with a firm brush using a little soap, then rinse. Grate on the fine mesh of your grater or use a zester.

Oranges

These are generally sweet, although some have a sharper flavour than others. Always choose eating oranges for juicing; Seville (Temple) oranges are too bitter. Blood oranges are sweeter than regular oranges and produce a lovely ruby-red juice.

Oranges are often used to make a base juice to which other juices can be added. To tone down the sweetness of orange juice, add grapefruit juice or dilute with water. Orange juice goes well with most other juices, particularly carrot, and can make a good base for smoothies too.

Therapeutic uses Orange juice is often used as a cold and flu remedy. It is rich in folic acid, which is good for cardiovascular health. It is recommended that women planning to conceive and those in the early stages of pregnancy have a good intake of folic acid in their diet (but supplements should also be taken to achieve the RDA at this time).

Grapefruits

Larger than oranges, grapefruits provide more juice. Their taste ranges from bitter/sour to sour/sweet. They add a mildly sour note to other sweeter juices, such as mango. Pink grapefruits are sweeter than yellow grapefruits.

Above: Vibrant pink grapefruits are sweeter than yellow ones.

Below: Buy oranges in bulk as they make a useful base juice.

Above: Refreshing clementines work as an effective digestive cleanser.

Therapeutic uses Grapefruit juice is thought to be useful in helping to lower cholesterol. It needs to be avoided if you are taking certain medications, particularly calcium-channel blockers and some chemotherapies. Consult your medical practitioner for advice.

Lemons and Limes

These fruits have a sour/bitter taste so are used only in small quantities. They are good with tomato juice, made into lemonade or limeade, or in a hot toddy – honey and lemon juice with hot water (and brandy or whisky if you like). The delicious zesty flavour works well with almost any combination of ingredients.

Therapeutic uses Lemons have antiseptic and antibacterial properties, and are traditionally used to support liver and kidney health. They are an alkaline fruit and are often used to help calm digestive acid.

Right: Blends can be livened up with a fresh squeeze of lemon or lime juice.

Mandarins, Tangerines, Satsumas, Clementines and Tangelos

These are all different crosses of citrus fruit. They have individual mild, aromatic sweetness, which varies with the type of fruit. None of them is as tart as oranges. They make good base juices and combine well with tropical fruit.

Therapeutic uses These fruits have similar properties to oranges and are also good digestive cleansers.

Other Citrus Fruits

Kumquat These can be fairly bitter, so juice them with intensely sweet ingredients, such as apricots. Slices of kumquat may also be used to decorate glasses.

GIVE ME FIVE!

Most governments agree that we need to eat five portions of fruit and vegetables a day, but many people are not sure what constitutes a "portion". Put simply, the daily total should come to 400g/14oz, so a portion is 80g/just under 3oz. A portion can be:

• one apple, one orange, one banana or another similar-sized fruit or vegetable
• two small fruits, such as tangerines or kiwi fruit
• half a large fruit, such as a grapefruit, or a generous slice of melon
• a small bowl of salad or fruit salad
• one cup of chopped vegetables
• one wine-glass full of fruit or vegetable juice (but remember that juice only counts towards one portion, so you can't drink juice all day and count it as five).

Note Potatoes do not count as a portion of vegetables because they are a starchy food.

Mineola This fruit is distinguished by a bump at its stem end. It has very few pips (seeds) and is wonderfully sweet, so is perfect for juicing.

Pomelos These are a type of orange with a sharp grapefruit flavour. Their slightly dry texture renders less juice than oranges, lemons or grapefruits, but their juice makes a good addition to mixed drinks that need sharpening.

Ugli fruit Named for its appearance, this fruit is delicious, mild, acid-sweet and juicy.

Orchard and stone fruit

Apples and pears are the classic orchard fruits and they are excellent for juicing. They are available year round and are relatively cheap, making them ideal to use as base juices. Other stone and orchard fruit, such as apricots, cherries and plums, are restricted to the summer season and tend to be more expensive, but they make deliciously sweet juices. Apples and pears store well in cool, dry conditions, but it is best to keep soft fruit in the refrigerator. All of these fruits are rich in vitamins and minerals, with apricots being particularly high in betacarotene – a natural source of vitamin A.

Preparing and Juicing Orchard and Stone Fruits

To juice orchard and stone fruits, you will need either a juicer for hard fruits, such as apples and pears, or a blender or food processor for softer fruits, such as peaches or plums. You will also need a chopping board and a sharp knife. A cherry stoner is useful for removing stones (pits) from cherries.

Hard fruits Apples, hard pears and quinces are best prepared with a juicer (centrifugal or masticating). Using a brush, scrub the skin with soap or washing-up liquid (dishwashing detergent) and water. Quarter the fruits and remove stems, but leave the core intact (although you can remove this if you prefer). Push the quarters through the juicer. Firmer peaches, nectarines or plums can also be put through a juicer, although the yield is much less than if blended. Halve or quarter these fruits and remove the stones.

Soft fruits Ripe apricots, cherries, peaches, nectarines, plums and greengages are best prepared in a blender or food processor as they produce a deliciously thick pulp. Halve or quarter these fruits, removing the stems and stones. There is no need to peel these fruits, though leaving the peel on will give the blend a thicker texture. If you do not peel the fruit, wash it thoroughly first.

Cherries These need to be pitted and this is most easily done using a cherry pitter.

To use a blender Place the fruit in the goblet and add your choice of liquid – water, juice, milk or milk substitute. Cover and select the appropriate speed. For a thicker consistency, add banana, yogurt or cream.

To use a food processor Place the prepared fruit in the bowl, cover and select the appropriate speed. The resulting pulp can be diluted to drinking consistency by adding water, a liquid juice such as apple or orange juice, milk or a milk substitute. If your food processor can crush ice, add some cubes at the end to create a lovely fruit "slush" drink.

CLASSIC COMBINATIONS

In the late summer and autumn, there is often a glut of locally grown orchard fruit or berries. Buy plenty and either freeze them for use later in the year, or juice them, taking advantage of some of these classic flavour combinations.

- **Apple and blackberry** – the sweetness of the apples offsets the tart blackberries perfectly.
- **Apple and carrot** – this juice is packed full of healthy nutrients.
- **Pear, melon and ginger** – the warmth of ginger complements the cool melon in this exotic blend.
- **Peach and apricot** – this thick blend can be thinned with sparkling mineral water.
- **Nectarine and cherry** – a delicious sweet blend that children will love.
- **Pear and cranberry** – this refreshing juice should be served with plenty of crushed ice.
- **Pear and apricot** – the thick, sweet apricot juice complements the subtle, aromatic flavour of pear.

Above: Apples make juice that can be very sweet, tangy or sour.

Apple

Depending on the type of apple, the taste will range from sweet to tart or sour. For juicing purposes choose eating apples, not cooking or crab apples. Apples are available all year round, making them ideal as a base juice to which other juices can be added. Apple juice oxidizes quickly to a brown colour but a little lemon juice will slow down this process.

Some classic juice combinations are apple and cranberry, apple and blackcurrant, and apple and carrot. While it may seem that choosing sweet apples is best, sharper tasting eating varieties are often better, as juicing concentrates the sweetness. They also balance out sweeter ingredients – for instance, sharp green apples work well to counterbalance the flavour of intensely sweet watermelon.

Therapeutic uses Apples are a good all-round fruit. They contain malic acid, which aids digestion, and they are high in pectin, a soluble fibre that helps to lower cholesterol and may help in the treatment of constipation and diarrhoea. If you want to detox and generally clear out your system, apples are the perfect fruit. Some varieties are also very rich in vitamin C, so they can help to boost the immune system and stave off winter colds and flu.

Pears

These fruits have an aromatic scent and delicate flavour, which comes out particularly well when they are juiced. To fully enjoy their subtle flavour it is best not to mix them with other very strong tasting juices, although they can be used to tone down the sometimes overwhelming flavours of cabbage and celery, for example.

Therapeutic uses This is another detoxifying fruit, which also provides an energizing boost. The levulose sugar in pears is more easily tolerated by diabetics than other sugars.

Apricots

If you can, choose tree-ripened fruit as the betacarotene levels increase by 200 per cent in the final ripening period. When blended, apricots produce a thick, rich pulp that is best when diluted with other more liquid juices such as cucumber, apple or carrot. Alternatively,

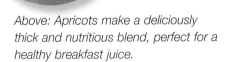

Above: Apricots make a deliciously thick and nutritious blend, perfect for a healthy breakfast juice.

you could thin the juice with a splash of sparkling mineral water or add natural (plain) yogurt to make a delicious smoothie. Dried apricots can be prepared in a blender with some water.

Therapeutic uses Apricots are particularly rich in betacarotene, one of the most important antioxidants, while dried apricots are a useful source of iron, potassium and fibre.

Above: Aromatic pears make a subtle and refreshing juice.

Above: Fresh cherries have a short season so enjoy them while you can.

Cherries

Choose ripe, sweet cherries for juicing as they do not ripen further after picking. They should be plump and firm, but not hard. Cherries lend a rich, aromatic flavour to juices and smoothies. Preparing them can be extremely time-consuming, and it helps if you have a cherry stoner to pit them. They are best used in small quantities with other blends and they turn juices and drinks a vibrant pinky-red colour. Cherry juice combines well with most other fruits and vegetables.

Therapeutic uses Powerhouses of the phyto (plant) nutrients proanthocyanins, which derive from their red colour, cherries have potent antioxidant characteristics. They also have painkilling abilities, which some people find particularly useful for relieving rheumatism. The pain relief characteristics can also be useful for alleviating headaches – a portion of 20 cherries is reputed to be the equivalent of one aspirin in terms of painkilling ability. Fresh cherries are also traditionally used to alleviate gout by helping to moderate uric acid levels. If you cannot find fresh cherries, the canned variety make a good substitute.

Peaches and Nectarines

These fruits produce similar thick, sweet juices, with peach juice being a little sweeter than that made with nectarines – but this difference is hardly noticeable once the juice has been blended.

Peaches have a fuzzy skin, which you may prefer to peel off before juicing, but this is not necessary. It is a bit of a waste putting peaches and nectarines

Above: Juice from plums can be slightly sour if the fruit is underripe.

Left: Nectarines do not need to be peeled before blending, but the large stone must be removed.

Above: Prunes add sweet flavour to juices when whizzed up in a blender.

through a juicer as a much better yield can be achieved using a blender or food processor. This process retains the fibre of the fruit, resulting in a much thicker, fruit purée, which can then be thinned if you like. If a recipe calls for fresh apricots but it is the wrong season and you cannot find them, peaches or nectarines make a good substitute.

Therapeutic uses Rich in vitamin C, betacarotene and other antioxidants, peaches and nectarines are excellent for skin, lung and digestive health, and are also particularly good for your eyes. One fresh nectarine contains an adult's entire recommended daily allowance of vitamin C. These fruits are very easy to digest but have a gentle laxative and diuretic effect, so should always be eaten in moderation.

Plums, Greengages, Damsons and Prunes

Plums and greengages have a sweet, refreshing taste, although some varieties, especially if unripe, can be a little bit tart. Greengages are incredibly sweet and perfect for juicing, while damsons are fairly sour with a strong flavour, so are generally cooked with sugar before using. Prunes are dried plums and are intensely sweet – they can be blended with water to make a thick sweet juice, and they combine well with most citrus fruits.

As with other sweet, soft fruit, plums are best used with other fruits that are less sweet or with more liquid ingredients, such as slightly sour apple juice. If plums are a little underripe, they will work well with extremely sweet fruits, such as bananas, mangoes or even orange juice.

Therapeutic uses Plums and prunes are known for their laxative properties. They are also very rich in potent antioxidants, making them a good choice for general health. Plums are a rich source of vitamin E and are good for maintaining healthy skin.

Quinces

These are an old-fashioned fruit but they are now becoming increasingly available throughout the year. Apple or pear-like in shape, depending on the variety, and with a pale golden colour, they have a delightful scented taste when cooked, but when eaten raw the flavour can be very astringent.

Quinces are hard when grown in cooler climates but ripen to a much softer texture when grown in warm climates. Although they are most often used in jellies and jams, for juicing purposes quinces should be prepared like apples, and are juiced in the same way. They should ideally be combined with a very sweet juice, such as peach or apricot, to counteract their tart, slightly bitter taste.

Therapeutic uses Elixir of quince was traditionally used, many years ago, to help invalids through long periods of convalescence.

Above: If you find fresh quinces, prepare them as you would apples and juice them in the same way, then combine with very sweet fruit juices such as mango or peach.

DRIED FRUIT

These are widely available and include raisins, sultanas (golden raisins) and currants, apricots, prunes, figs, mangoes, papaya, banana, apple rings and dates. Dried fruits do not juice well because they are dehydrated; however, they can be rehydrated by soaking in hot water, tea (Earl Grey is delicious), warmed wine or fortified wine. Adding cinnamon or another spice, such as cloves, complements their flavour. Dried fruits provide more concentrated sources of nutrients – including iron, magnesium and antioxidants – than their fresh equivalents. They are very sweet, so a little goes a long way in juices and blended drinks.

Above: Semi-dried apricots do not need soaking before use.

Above: Clockwise from top left, sultanas, currants and raisins don't juice well, but can be finely chopped and added to smoothies or fruit blends.

Berries and currants

Tiny delicious currants and ripe berries are ideal for making smoothies and shakes. You will need a blender or a food processor for this because soft fruits do not go through juicers well. Berries are mainly a summer fruit and this is when they not only taste their best but are also cheapest, although they are often available at other times of the year when they are imported. They must be stored in the refrigerator and used within two days of purchase at most. Berries need careful handling and you need to watch them as they can quickly become overripe. If you cannot find fresh berries and currants, frozen ones are a good option.

Weight for weight, strawberries, raspberries and blackcurrants contain as much vitamin C as citrus fruits. Dark red berries are also rich sources of proanthocyanins, which are powerful antioxidants. Some people have an allergic reaction to strawberries and other berries, especially if they eat too many, and this can result in a strawberry rash or even a fever.

FREEZING FRUIT
If there is a glut of berries you can freeze them for blending at other times of the year.

Remove the stalks and leaves, then place the fruit on a baking sheet in a single layer to freeze. Once frozen transfer to a freezerproof container or bag. When you want to use them, either defrost first or blend from frozen for an iced effect.

Preparing and Blending Berries and Currants
To juice berries and currants, you will need either a blender or a food processor, a chopping board and a small, sharp knife.

Soft fruits These are easy to prepare for blending. Rinse, if you like, then discard any overripe or mouldy fruit. Remove any stems and leaves, either pulling them off by hand or using a sharp knife. Remove the calyx from strawberries, but remember there is no need to hull them when making juices.

To use a blender Place the prepared soft fruits in the flask, add liquid, such as water, fruit juice, milk or milk substitute, cover and select the appropriate speed. Add banana, other soft fruits, yogurt or cream to make a thicker consistency.

To use a food processor Place the prepared fruit in the bowl, cover and process. If you prefer a thinner consistency, the resulting pulp can be diluted by adding mineral water (still or sparkling, depending on your preference), a liquid juice such as orange juice, milk or a milk substitute.

Adding ice Create a delicious berry ice crush by adding plenty of ice to the blend. Before crushing ice in a blender of food processor, however, check the manufacturer's instructions.

MAKING A FRUIT COULIS
Coulis make delicious, jewel-coloured additions to trickle over a smoothie or milkshake, or even an ice cream, before serving.

1 Choose one fruit depending on the colour or flavour you want: raspberries or strawberries for dark red or pinkish red, peeled kiwi fruit for bright green or soaked dried apricots for a vibrant orange colour.

2 Put the fruit in a blender – approximately one small handful per person should be enough. Blend on high speed until puréed. If using dried apricots you will need to add 15–30ml/1–2 tbsp water before blending to achieve the correct consistency.

3 Strain the raspberry or strawberry coulis if you want a seedless purée.

Above: Buy plenty of strawberries for juicing when they are in season.

Strawberries, Raspberries, Blackberries and Mulberries

Generally sweet but with a sharp undertone, strawberries are at their best and sweetest when perfectly ripe. Wild strawberries are much smaller than cultivated strawberries and have an intense, delicious flavour, but they are generally too expensive to blend unless you are lucky enough to have your own supply. Buy brightly coloured, plump berries and do not wash them until you are ready to use them.

Raspberries are a delicate berry so handle them with care, giving them just a light rinse, if necessary. They are more tart tasting than strawberries and they add a deeper reddish colour than the light pinky colour that strawberries give. Try a classic strawberry milkshake or a raspberry and peach smoothie to sample these fruits at their best.

Blackberries arrive later in the summer season than other berries, usually just as autumn is approaching. They grow wild in the countryside in abundance, but you can also find cultured blackberries in large supermarkets. They are very sweet and juicy when fully ripe.

Mulberries look a bit like blackberries in size and shape but they are less widely available. When ripe, their flavour is sweet but slightly sour and they are less aromatic than other berries.

When in season these fruits will be reasonably priced and you could use them as a base juice, but at other times, when the fruit is more expensive, just a few berries will add a really distinctive taste and colour to drinks. They blend well with bananas, orange juice, apples, melons, peaches and most other delicately flavoured fruits. Blackberries will dominate the colour of most other juices, turning the blend a deep, dark purple, but the taste is subtle enough to mix well with most fruit and vegetable combinations. Blackberries go particularly well with apples – a classic combination.

Therapeutic uses Strawberries are rich in pectin and ellagic acid, which makes them excellent for cleansing and detoxification. All four berries are good sources of proanthocyanins and have lots of vitamin C, both of which are good for boosting the immune system. As an antioxidant, vitamin C may even reduce the risk of developing certain cancers. Berries are a valuable source of calcium, which is important for healthy bones and teeth, and they are also soothing for the nervous system. People with cardiovascular health problems should include berries in their diet for their antioxidant properties. Raspberry juice is believed to cleanse the digestive system, and raspberries have traditionally been used in the treatment of diarrhoea, indigestion and rheumatism.

Above: Raspberries add a delicious tart flavour and a vibrant red colour.

Right: Hunt for wild blackberry bushes, then pick your own.

Above: The intense colour of blueberries will dominate any blend you add them to.

Blueberries

Also called bilberries, blueberries are very sweet when ripe, but rather tart when underripe. Generally, they have a short summer season, though in warm countries the season is prolonged. Buy plenty and freeze them in small bags.

As with blackberries, the dark juice of blueberries will dominate the blend; in this case the juice is a rich bluish-purple. They are a delicious addition to most fruit blends or, if you prefer simple juices, just add sparkling mineral water to a thick blueberry purée.

Therapeutic uses Blueberries are one of the most potent fruits in terms of antioxidant power. Primarily used to boost the immune system, they also play an important role in eye health. During World War II, pilots ate blueberries because they believed it would improve their night vision. As with cranberries, they are good for relieving urinary tract infections.

Blackcurrants, Redcurrants and Whitecurrants

The general flavour of blackcurrants is sour-sweet, depending on how ripe they are. They are best sweetened, although this is not necessary if you are mixing a small amount of blackcurrant juice with a sweeter fruit juice. They make ideal mixers but they are not good juiced on their own. Blackcurrants are more often made into cordials than into juices, and you could add some cordial to a juice made of other fruits.

Redcurrants and whitecurrants are available at the same time of the year as blackcurrants but are less abundant and can be more difficult to find. They are good mixed with less expensive blackcurrants in juices and smoothies.

Therapeutic uses Few fruits and vegetables have more vitamin C than blackcurrants, making them powerful allies in wintertime for fending off colds and flu. Blackcurrant pips (seeds) are a rich source of essential fatty acids (the same as those in evening primrose oil), which are helpful for female hormonal health, relieving symptoms of pre-menstrual syndrome and mastalgia (sore breasts).

Left: Whitecurrants are sweeter than other currants and less tart.

Left: Mix redcurrants with sweeter ingredients for a delicious blend.

Above: Tart blackcurrants contain more vitamin C than almost any other fruit, but are best used in small quantities.

*Above:
Cranberries mix
well with sweet orchard
fruits, such as pear.*

berry is too tiny and sour for juicing, but makes an excellent sweet syrup when boiled with sugar and water. Elderflower syrup is a traditional immune-boosting remedy. In spring and early summer, the flowers are gathered and can be used to make delicious and fragrant elderflower cordial.

Cranberries

These lovely berries are associated with the winter season as they are generally not available fresh at other times of the year. Buy them when available and keep them in your freezer until needed. Cranberries are fairly sour and need to be sweetened. They work well with juice made from sweet oranges, apples, pears or with carrot in a ratio of a quarter cranberry juice to three-quarters of the sweeter ingredient.

Therapeutic uses Cranberries are very successful at preventing or resolving cystitis and other urinary tract infections when drunk as a juice over several days. The antioxidants they contain specifically target the bacteria of the urinary tract and prevent them from adhering and causing damage. The quinine contained in cranberries is an effective liver detoxifier.

Other Berries

Elderberries These are not generally available in the shops but must be gathered from the wild. The elder tree grows widely and can be found in many urban gardens. It is not uncommon for people to disregard it as a weed. The

Gooseberries These have a short summer season but can be frozen on baking sheets. They are widely available but not often used for juicing because they can be extremely sour. However, you could add a small number to a juice to gain the benefit of their immune-supporting effects.

Below: Instead of juicing raw, elderberries are first boiled with sugar to make a syrup.

SUMMER SMOOTHIES
When there is a glut of surplus berries but you don't want to freeze them, try making some of these classic berry smoothies.

- **Raspberry and orange** – this smoothie has a delicious tart flavour and is perfect for breakfast.
- **Cranberry and pear** – sweet and juicy pear contrasts with the slightly dry flavour of cranberries.
- **Summer fruits** – simply redcurrants, raspberries, strawberries and blackberries.
- **Redcurrant and cranberry** – a tart and refreshing smoothie, perfect on a summer's day.
- **Raspberry and apple** – kids will love this combination with plenty of crushed ice.
- **Blueberry and orange** – this smoothie will take on a vibrant bluish-purple colour.
- **Blackberry and cinnamon** – a warm, spicy blend guaranteed to impress guests.

*Left: Freeze
gooseberries to
use all year
round.*

Exotic and other fruits

Most exotic fruits are now available year round. These fruits are mainly blended because, apart from melons and pineapples, they will not go through a juicer very well. Melons, pineapples and bananas produce enough juice to use as base ingredients, but the availability and yield of other exotic fruits mean that they are best used in smaller quantities. Orange-coloured fruits, such as mangoes, are excellent sources of betacarotene.

Preparing and Juicing Exotic and Other Fruits

You will need a blender or food processor, a juicer (centrifugal or masticating), a chopping board and a sharp knife. A spoon is useful for scooping the flesh out of some fruits.

Melons Cut a wedge and scoop out the pips (seeds). Cut away the flesh and purée in a blender or food processor. Firmer melons can be put through a juicer, particularly watermelon.

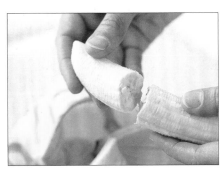

Bananas Peel and then break the flesh into chunks. Put the banana into a blender or food processor and blend to a pulp, then add other fruit juice until you get the right consistency.

Pineapples Lie the pineapple on its side on a chopping board, then, using a large sharp knife, slice off the base and the top. Cut the fruit into thick slices, then remove the skin. The flesh can be put in a blender or food processor, or pushed through a juicer.

Kiwi fruit, papaya and guava Cut the fruit in half. For papaya and guava, scoop out the seeds. For all three fruits, either scoop out the ripe flesh with a spoon or peel with a sharp knife. Put the flesh in a blender or food processor. None of these yields enough juice when put through a juicer.

Mangoes Slice down either side of the stone. Score the flesh into small squares, then push the skin from the outside and cut off the flesh into a blender or food processor.

Lychees The easiest way to peel lychees is by hand; the skin is slightly stiff and cracks easily. Ease the fruit out and remove the stone. Put the flesh in a blender or food processor. Lychees do not yield enough juice in a juicer.

RHUBARB

Traces of oxalic acid, which inhibits calcium and iron absorption and may exacerbate joint problems, can be found in many vegetables. The high levels of oxalic acid in rhubarb mean that it should not be used raw, and rhubarb leaves should never be eaten because they are poisonous. Rhubarb can, however, be added to drinks if it is cooked first. It contains high levels of calcium, potassium and thiamine (vitamin B_1).

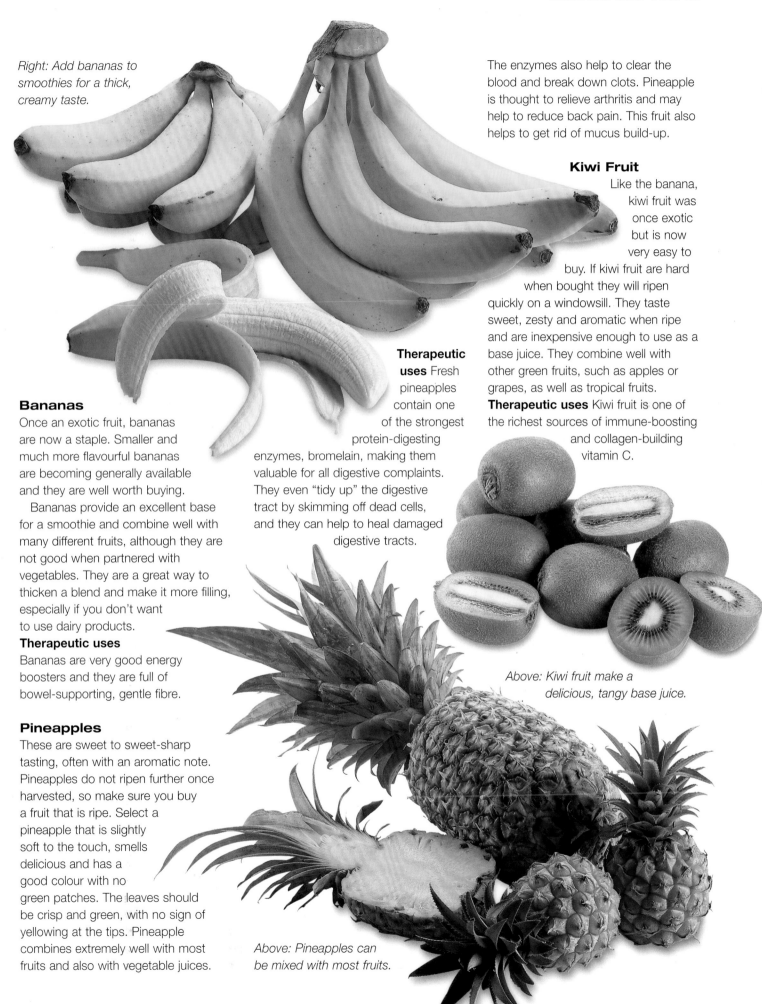

Right: Add bananas to smoothies for a thick, creamy taste.

The enzymes also help to clear the blood and break down clots. Pineapple is thought to relieve arthritis and may help to reduce back pain. This fruit also helps to get rid of mucus build-up.

Kiwi Fruit

Like the banana, kiwi fruit was once exotic but is now very easy to buy. If kiwi fruit are hard when bought they will ripen quickly on a windowsill. They taste sweet, zesty and aromatic when ripe and are inexpensive enough to use as a base juice. They combine well with other green fruits, such as apples or grapes, as well as tropical fruits.

Therapeutic uses Kiwi fruit is one of the richest sources of immune-boosting and collagen-building vitamin C.

Therapeutic uses Fresh pineapples contain one of the strongest protein-digesting enzymes, bromelain, making them valuable for all digestive complaints. They even "tidy up" the digestive tract by skimming off dead cells, and they can help to heal damaged digestive tracts.

Bananas

Once an exotic fruit, bananas are now a staple. Smaller and much more flavourful bananas are becoming generally available and they are well worth buying.

Bananas provide an excellent base for a smoothie and combine well with many different fruits, although they are not good when partnered with vegetables. They are a great way to thicken a blend and make it more filling, especially if you don't want to use dairy products.

Therapeutic uses
Bananas are very good energy boosters and they are full of bowel-supporting, gentle fibre.

Above: Kiwi fruit make a delicious, tangy base juice.

Pineapples

These are sweet to sweet-sharp tasting, often with an aromatic note. Pineapples do not ripen further once harvested, so make sure you buy a fruit that is ripe. Select a pineapple that is slightly soft to the touch, smells delicious and has a good colour with no green patches. The leaves should be crisp and green, with no sign of yellowing at the tips. Pineapple combines extremely well with most fruits and also with vegetable juices.

Above: Pineapples can be mixed with most fruits.

Left: Ripe mangoes have extremely soft flesh that is juicy and sweet.

Above: Aromatic lychees contain significant amounts of vitamin C.

Mangoes, Papayas and Guavas

These fruits are best bought ripe, when they yield slightly to gentle pressure, which is when they are at their sweetest. They are all aromatic, delicious and luxurious tasting. They combine well with banana and orange juice, apples or carrot to make tasty tropical smoothies.

Therapeutic uses Papaya is distinguished by its potent digestive enzyme, papain, which has all the advantages of bromelain (see pineapples). Papain also has a reputation for helping to restore healthy bowel flora (bacterial balance). All three fruits are rich in betacarotene and contain generous amounts of vitamin C as well as many minerals, making them excellent all-round sources of nutrition.

Lychees

These have a subtle, aromatic and sweet taste. They need to be combined with equally delicately flavoured fruits so that their flavour is not lost. Combine them in smoothie blends with melons, bananas, apples or strawberries.

Therapeutic uses Lychees are a good source of vitamin C.

Right: The juice from Galia melons is delicious when combined with either fruit or vegetables.

Melons

There are many different types of melon available, including cantaloupe, honeydew and watermelon. They are members of the gourd family, which also includes cucumbers and squashes. To choose a ripe melon (apart from watermelon), press the blossom end, which should yield slightly to gentle pressure. A ripe melon will have a sweet, perfumed aroma. For watermelon, tap the side of the fruit, which should sound hollow; the rind should barely give when pressed with a thumb.

Melons make a sweet, refreshing base juice that combines well with other fruits, such as tart apples or pears, or with slightly bitter vegetables such as cabbage.

Therapeutic uses Melons have a diuretic and digestive cleansing action, and they are good for all problem skin conditions. The pips (seeds) are very rich in potassium, which helps to lower high blood pressure, and they are also valued for their zinc and vitamin E content, so it is worthwhile including a few. All of the orange-fleshed melons are rich in betacarotene, which is good for the immune system and for eye health in general. Watermelon also provides the phytonutrient lycopene, which is reputedly powerful in fighting against certain types of cancer, including prostate cancer. Lycopene must be consumed together with a small amount of fat to facilitate absorption, and supplements are recommended to gain its full benefit.

Grapes

Depending on the variety, grapes can be sweet or tart tasting. Black, red, green (or white) grapes are available, and you can choose from seeded or seedless varieties. They produce a light green or pink juice depending on the colour of the grape.

Grapes are fairly watery so they work well with fruits that produce thicker juice, such as mangoes, papayas, peaches or plums. They are a useful and delicious addition to most fruit and vegetable juices.

Therapeutic uses Dark-skinned grapes are rich in a compound called resveratrol, one of the most potent antioxidants, as well as proanthocyanins, and all colours of grapes have high levels of ellagic acid, which is a potent detoxifier. Grape juice is a traditional naturopathic rest cure and is also sometimes used as a nerve tonic. Grapes have been reported to help alleviate the symptoms of arthritis.

Right: There is no need to remove grape pips before blending as they will just be incorporated into the juice.

TROPICAL TOPPERS

Some tropical fruits are not good for juicing as they either yield too little juice or are too fiddly to prepare. Try using them as pretty decorations and toppings.

Figs Cut from the pointed end downwards but do not cut right through the base. Make a second cut at right angles to the first, creating a cross shape. Squeeze the fruit gently to open up into a "flower". This makes an attractive edible decoration – eat them with the skin on. Figs do not yield much juice but you can combine them with other juices. They have a strong laxative action, so should be consumed in moderation, and are useful for irritated bronchial tubes.

Star fruit (carambola) These pretty tropical fruits can be sliced very thinly into attractive star-shaped decorations.

Pomegranates Cut these in half and scoop out the scarlet pips (seeds), separating them from the pith. Sweet, refreshing and crunchy, the pips are ideal for sprinkling on top of juices and smoothies.

Passion fruit Cut in half and scoop out the pulp and pips (seeds). Sweet, aromatic and attractive, this pulp makes an ideal juice topping.

Dates Cut dates in half and discard the stone (pit). Although they cannot be juiced, they can be chopped and added to blends. Otherwise, slice thinly and serve as a side snack with a drink.

Root and tuber vegetables

These vegetables must be juiced using a centrifugal or masticating juicer. Carrot is the only root vegetable that is suitable to be used as a base juice, but others can be included in smaller proportions in juices and blends. Root vegetables are essentially autumnal and winter vegetables, but they are generally available year round. They all store best in cool, dry conditions, although beetroot (beet) is best kept in the refrigerator.

Preparing and Juicing Root and Tuber Vegetables

To juice root and tuber vegetables, you will need an electric juicer (centrifugal or masticating), a scrubbing brush or a vegetable peeler, a chopping board and a sharp knife.

Peeling When preparing root and tuber vegetables, decide first if you are going to peel them or just scrub off the dirt. With many fruits and vegetables it is a shame to peel them as a good proportion of the nutrients are just under the skin. Your decision will be, in part, influenced by how thin the skin is. You may want to peel old and gnarled carrots but leave small new carrots unpeeled. You do not usually need to peel carrots, beetroot (beet), celeriac, parsnips, radishes, swedes (rutabaga), turnips, sweet potatoes or yams. While you can include potato skin, you must be sure to cut away any peel or flesh that is sprouting or green in any way. This green colour indicates the presence of a highly toxic alkaloid called solanine, which could cause illness.

Juicing When root vegetables are juiced they tend to produce foam, which settles at the top of the juice. This can taste a bit earthy (even when the vegetables have been scrubbed clean). However, this taste indicates their high mineral content so the topping should be drunk for maximum benefit (you can mix it in with the rest of the juice). If you find the taste particularly unpleasant, just spoon it off, but do not strain the juice.

Carrot

When juiced, carrots are very sweet and the fresh juice has a much better flavour than commercial carrot juice. Because they yield a lot of mild-tasting juice, carrots provide the basis for many combinations. They work very well with both vegetables and fruit.

Therapeutic uses Rich in betacarotene, which is good for the immune system as well as for skin and eye health.

Nursing mothers are sometimes advised to drink carrot juice; it contains more easily assimilated calcium than cow's milk, which is essential to healthy growth in infancy. To ensure that betacarotene is converted to vitamin A (a fat-soluble vitamin) as needed, it helps to add 5ml/1 tsp flax seed oil or walnut oil to the carrot juice, or some full cream (whole) or semi-skimmed (low-fat) milk.

Beetroot

A rich ruby-red colour is imparted to drinks by the inclusion of beetroot (beet). Always used raw, they do not need to be peeled, just scrubbed. The juice is quite strong tasting, so use it sparingly: about one quarter beetroot juice to three-quarters other juice.

Beetroot greens enhance the nutritional value of the juice. However, they are fairly high in oxalic acid, which is poisonous if consumed in large quantities. Juiced beetroot and leaves work well in all vegetable combinations.

Therapeutic uses Beetroot is used as a blood fortifier and iron builder in traditional herbalism, particularly for heavy menstrual blood loss. It is very rich in immune-boosting beta-carotene, as well as many other minerals, including iron and manganese. It is also traditionally used during convalescence.

Above: Carrots make a sweet juice that works well as a base when combined with juice from other fruits or vegetables.

Right: Beetroot provides a stunning deep red juice.

Parsnip

This vegetable is high in sugar and so, like carrots, tastes fairly sweet. The juice is also quite creamy tasting. However, unlike carrot juice, parsnip juice should be added in smaller quantities – about one quarter parsnip to three-quarters other juice. It works best with other vegetable juices, especially slightly spicy, peppery ones.

Therapeutic uses Parsnips have a settling effect on the stomach and are mildly diuretic. Rich in silicon, they are also good for hair, skin and nails.

Radish

These attractive vegetables come in a variety of shapes and sizes. They have a distinctive peppery taste, so use them in small quantities as a flavouring for other vegetable juices. They are ideal for bringing a bland juice to life.

Therapeutic uses As with any peppery vegetable, radishes have a tonic effect on the liver and gall bladder. They also help to clear the sinuses.

Sweet Potatoes and Yams

Although these two vegetables look similar, they are not actually related and yams tend to be drier than sweet potatoes. There are many varieties of sweet potato, with flesh ranging from pale yellow to a vivid orange. Yam flesh varies from off-white, to yellow and pink, or even purple. Choose unblemished, smooth produce and store in a dark, cool, dry place.

Above: Peppery radishes should be juiced in small quantities only.

Therapeutic uses Both of these tubers are high in starch, with yams containing more natural sugar then sweet potatoes, but with a lower vitamin A and C content. They are both energizing and easier to digest than standard potatoes and they have an alkalizing effect on the body, which helps to curb over-acidity. Some people believe that they have anti-carcinogenic properties.

Celeriac, Swedes and Turnips

Celeriac has a mild celery taste; swede (rutabaga) is sweet and creamy but slightly earthy tasting; and turnips taste mild and peppery. Most of the nutrients in turnips are concentrated in the tops, so juice them along with the stems and leaves instead of discarding them. All of these vegetables work best when added to other vegetable blends, for example in a carrot-based juice with green leafy vegetables, but they do not combine particularly well with fruit.

Therapeutic uses Celeriac has a mildly astringent, diuretic action, while swede is energizing. Turnips, with their tops, provide a good source of calcium (without the limiting oxalic acid found in beetroot (beet) and spinach), making them a good nerve tonic, and they are also thought to be useful when you are feeling run down or depressed. By weight, turnip tops contain twice as much vitamin C as citrus fruit, and they also have an expectorant action, which is useful for chesty coughs.

Potatoes

Any type of potato can be used, but you must always use them raw in blended drinks. Potato is not a juice that anybody would drink on its own, but it has a slightly nutty flavour that is not unpleasant when mixed with other vegetable juices. It does, however, have good therapeutic effects, which makes it worth including. You only need a small quantity mixed with another juice, such as carrot, at a ratio of about one-eighth potato to seven-eighths other juice. (See the important note about preparation of potatoes opposite.)

Therapeutic uses Potato peel is high in potassium and may help to lower blood pressure, while the juice has traditionally been used to treat stomach ulcers and arthritis.

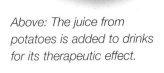

Above: The juice from potatoes is added to drinks for its therapeutic effect.

Leafy and brassica vegetables

Green leafy vegetables and brassicas need to be juiced using a juicer. The brassica family includes broccoli, cauliflower, and Brussels sprouts. Ideally these, and all leafy vegetables, should be stored in the refrigerator to avoid wilting, yellowing or browning, and they are best used as soon as possible after purchase as they quickly lose their nutritional value. They are all used in small quantities, to add flavour or for their nutritional or therapeutic properties, with other bulkier base juices. Generally you will add one quarter juice made from green leaves to three-quarters juice made from other ingredients.

All dark green leafy vegetables are good sources of magnesium and betacarotene, and many are also rich in iron. This group has important health qualities. They are all rich in compounds such as sulphurophanes, which are responsible for the vegetables' slightly bitter taste, and indole-3-carbinol, which is believed to have cancer-inhibiting properties.

Preparing and Juicing Leafy and Brassica Vegetables

To juice leafy and brassica vegetables, you will need a juicer (centrifugal or masticating), a chopping board and a sharp knife.

Loose, leafy vegetables Separate out the leaves and wash thoroughly. Cut away any that are discoloured but keep the outer leaves as they are richer in nutrients than the interior ones. Do not discard the cores of lettuce or any leaf stems.

Tightly packed leaves Vegetables, such as chicory (Belgian endive) or Chinese leaves (Chinese cabbage), should be washed, then quartered or chopped into an appropriate size to pass through the neck of the machine. Cut broccoli and cauliflower into florets and wash the pieces thoroughly. The cores can also be juiced.

To extract the maximum juice It is best to alternate putting leaves through the machine with a hard vegetable or fruit such as carrot or apple. This keeps the machine working efficiently to extract the maximum juice.

Cabbages and Brussels Sprouts

Dark green cabbage is the best choice for juicing as it is nutrient-rich. White cabbage is its poor relation, nutritionally speaking. Red cabbage generally tastes better when cooked, but if it is used for juicing the lovely purple colour will dominate your blend. Cabbage lends a surprisingly light, green taste to juices as long as the quantity of cabbage used does not overwhelm the blend. About one-eighth to one-quarter cabbage is the right quantity in any juice. Brussels sprouts, which are really just mini-cabbages, taste similar to cabbages when juiced but are slightly more nutty.

Therapeutic uses Using the dark green, outer leaves is important if you want to obtain the maximum level of nutrients. Along with the rest of the brassica family, cabbages are regarded as anti-cancer vegetables. Cabbage juice is also a powerful gut and ulcer healer. It should not be used excessively by people with underactive thyroids because cabbages are known to be goitrogenous and interfere with thyroid function.

These and other leafy vegetables should also be eaten in moderation by people on blood-thinning medication, as they are high in the blood-clotting factor, vitamin K. Cabbages and Brussels sprouts provide the richest vegetable sources of vitamin C.

Spinach

This has a mild, slightly peppery taste and lends a delightful green colour to juices. It is used in small quantities to add taste and nutrients to other sweeter bases, including some milder fruits such as apples or pears.

Therapeutic uses Spinach is very nutritious, high in betacarotene and folic acid, and rich in vitamins A and C. Its iron content is good although not as high as was once believed. It also contains the phytochemicals xeaxanthin and lutein, which are known to protect the eyes against ageing.

Above: Brussels sprouts should be juiced in small quantities only.

Above: Known as a superfood, broccoli is packed with iron and vitamin C.

Cauliflower and Broccoli

These vegetables should have tightly packed, firm heads, showing no signs of wilt or discoloration. They are both available in more exotic forms, such as purple sprouting broccoli and cauliflower hybrids, and these can also be juiced, although these varieties can be expensive. Broccoli tastes slightly bitter while cauliflower is creamy. They are best used in small quantities with other milder flavours such as carrot or beetroot (beet).

Therapeutic uses Along with cabbage and Brussels sprouts, these are thought to be anti-cancer foods, and they are powerful additions to juices. They are not goitrogenous but are high in vitamin K. Broccoli is a good source of vitamin C.

Lettuce

There are many types of lettuce available. It is easier to juice firm rather than softer leaves. Most varieties lend a slightly bitter taste to juices, so should only be used in small quantities. It works well in either vegetable or fruit blends.

Therapeutic uses Lettuce is well known for its soporific, calming and sleep-inducing qualities. Very rich in asparagine, which is also found in asparagus, it has a slight laxative and digestive cleansing effect.

Kale and Watercress

Both of these vegetables are strong tasting; kale is slightly bitter while watercress has a peppery flavour, so add only small amounts to juices. They are best used alongside other vegetable juices.

Therapeutic uses Watercress and kale are nutrient powerhouses, and are used extensively in therapeutic juicing. Excellent sources of magnesium, calcium and iron, watercress is also rich in sulphur, which is good for the hair and nails.

Other Leafy Vegetables

There are many different types of leafy vegetables. Slightly bitter or peppery leaves include radicchio, rocket (arugula), Swiss chard, chicory (Belgian endive) and endive (US chicory). These are best when used in small quantities and mixed with other vegetable juices. Sweeter tasting leaves include Chinese leaves (Chinese cabbage) and pak choi (bok choy) – these combine well with both vegetable and fruit juices.

Above: All green-leafed vegetables are full of minerals and nutrients but should be mixed with other vegetables.

Therapeutic uses Leaves are excellent sources of minerals, and darker ones contain lots of carotenoids, which help to neutralize free radicals. Bitter-tasting leaves contain chemicals that are thought to have liver, gall bladder and digestive cleansing properties.

Wild Greens

Look around when you are out on a walk and you will be able to identify a number of wild greens. In times gone by everyone was familiar with these free foods and they were incorporated into many dishes. It is fairly easy to find dandelion, sorrel and nettles, and watercress can also be found in some areas. Before gathering these plants make sure you have identified them correctly and check that they have not been sprayed with weed killers.

Therapeutic uses Wild greens are traditionally used in tonics to cure anaemia. Dandelion leaves are used as a nerve tonic and also help to balance acid/alkaline levels, which makes them useful in arthritic conditions. Nettles are believed to be useful in combating the symptoms of hay fever, and they are also thought to be helpful in relieving rheumatism and settling nervous eczema.

Vegetable fruits

Some vegetables are actually the fruit of the plant, although they are not sweet in the way that we usually think of fruit. If allowed to ripen on the vine they are all exceptionally rich in various nutrients.

Preparing and Juicing Vegetable Fruits

You will need a chopping board, a sharp knife, a spoon, a fork, a blender or food processor and a juicer (masticating or centrifugal).

Preparing avocados Make sure the avocado is ripe and yields slightly to pressure applied to the skin. Cut the avocado in half lengthways, ease the two halves apart and scoop out the stone (pit) with a spoon. Scoop out the flesh and place it in a blender or food processor with other ingredients. (Avocados are too soft to put in a juicer.)

You could also mash the flesh using a fork and stir it into a blend by hand.

Juicing (bell) peppers Cut the pepper in half lengthways, then cut away the stem, pips (seeds) and pith. Wash under running water to remove any remaining pips, then push the flesh through a juicer.

Skinning tomatoes These can be juiced whole or skinned first. To skin tomatoes, place them in a heatproof bowl and pour boiling water over them. Leave to soak for 2–3 minutes. Lift the tomatoes out, nick the skin with the point of a knife and it should begin to peel back. Peel off the loosened skin. Blend the tomatoes in a blender or food processor.

Avocados

When properly ripe, avocados are rich and slightly nutty tasting. They lend a creamy texture to juices and can be used to thicken a blend as an alternative to milk. They combine well with most vegetable juices – adding a little lemon juice will help cut through the richness and will slow down discoloration.

Therapeutic uses Avocados are an excellent source of oleic acid, which is associated with heart health. They are also full of vitamin E, which is essential for healthy skin.

Peppers

Although they come in a variety of colours, (bell) peppers are all the same vegetable – green peppers are simply unripe red peppers. Peppers do not ripen much after picking, so they don't change colour or become sweeter. The taste of yellow, orange and red peppers is similarly sweet, while green ones have a slightly more bitter flavour.

Peppers can dominate a juice and so are best used in small quantities. They are ideal combined with tomato juice.

Therapeutic uses Peppers are one of the richest sources of vitamin C, so they provide support for the immune system. Yellow, orange and red peppers also contain high levels of the antioxidant betacarotene.

Below: Avocados contain plenty of vitamin E, making them good for the skin.

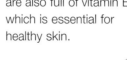

Tomatoes

Mild-tasting tomatoes are sweet when ripe and acidic when unripe. Select vine-ripened tomatoes for the best flavour. Tomatoes mix well with most other vegetables and fruits. They are often used as a base juice as they are abundant and versatile.

Therapeutic uses Tomatoes are a rich source of lycopene, which has stronger antioxidant properties than betacarotene. They are also thought to have anti-cancer properties.

Left: For the best flavour, store tomatoes at room temperature.

Squash vegetables

The high water content of these vegetables makes them ideal for juicing in a centrifugal or masticating juicer. Cucumbers are available all year round and the best variety to use for juicing is the English (hothouse) cucumber. Courgettes (zucchini) are also available all year round, but are at their best in the summer, and other squashes only appear in the autumn. Cucumbers and courgettes should be stored in the refrigerator, but other squashes may be kept for up to a week or two in cool, dry conditions.

Preparing and Juicing Squash Vegetables

To juice squash vegetables, you will need a juicer (either centrifugal or masticating), a clean chopping board and a sharp knife.

Preparing cucumbers and courgettes Wash the skin, using a scrubbing brush if the vegetables are waxed. There is no need to peel or seed them, but do so if you prefer. Cut into large chunks and push through the juicer. You could also blend cucumbers in a blender or food processor as they contain so much water.

Right: Courgette skin contains valuable nutrients so don't peel before juicing.

Juicing squashes Cut large squashes, such as butternut and pumpkin, in half and scoop out most of the pips (seeds), leaving some to go through the juicer, if you like. Slice away the peel, then cut the flesh into large chunks and push through the juicer.

Cucumber and Courgette

When juiced, all cucumbers are mild and tasty, although small cucumbers have the best flavour. Ideal for using as a base juice, they mix well with both vegetables and fruit. Courgettes (zucchini) are similar to cucumbers when juiced, but not quite as sweet.

Therapeutic uses The nutrients of cucumbers and courgettes are mainly concentrated in the skin, which is why you should leave it on. If this is too bitter, experiment with peeling half the skin. These vegetables have a strong diuretic action and help to lower high blood pressure. They support healthy hair and nail growth, and also help relieve the symptoms of rheumatism.

JUICY SOUP

Raw vegetable juices can be used very successfully as soups. Either enjoy them cold in the summer, garnished with a dollop of cream or yogurt and chopped fresh herbs, or warm them through (but do not boil) in the winter months.

Gazpacho, which is made with raw tomatoes, cucumber and (bell) peppers, is the classic soup made in this way.

Pumpkin and Butternut Squash

Both of these squashes produce a juice with a surprisingly sweet and nutty taste, but it is not a juice that you would want to drink on its own. Mix one-quarter pumpkin or squash juice with three-quarters other vegetable juice, such as carrot or cucumber, along with something else to give it a bit of a zing – perhaps a bit of onion.

Therapeutic uses Be sure to include some of the pips in the juice as they are high in zinc and iron. As with all the vegetables in this family they have a kidney-supporting and anti-water-retention action and are also powerhouses of carotenoid antioxidants.

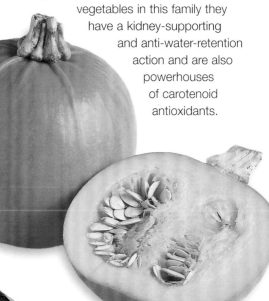

Above: Pumpkins produce a sweet, nutty juice that is best mixed with other flavours.

Pod, shoot and bulb vegetables

All of these vegetables need to be put through a juicer. They all produce fairly strong tasting juices which should be combined with other vegetables. Pods and bulbs share the common trait that they, along with seeds, are potential plants. This means that all the goodness for the growing plant is stored in the pod or bulb ready for use, so you get many extra nutritional benefits. Shoots are also highly nutritious because they are at the stage of growth before a fully-fledged plant develops – they are fantastically rich in nutritional power for the growing plant.

Preparing and Juicing Pod, Shoot and Bulb Vegetables

To juice pod, shoot and bulb vegetables, you will need a juicer (centrifugal or masticating), a chopping board and a sharp knife.

Preparing pods French (green) beans, broad (fava) beans, runner beans and mangetout (snow peas) do not need any preparation other than ensuring that they are clean. They do not require stringing or trimming as the juicer will simply turn the undesirable parts of the vegetables into pulp.

Preparing bulbs Pull off the outer leaves and wash these vegetables thoroughly before juicing, then cut into chunks the right size for your machine. It is not essential to remove the outer leaves or skin from onions, spring onions (scallions), leeks, fennel and celery, but they must be washed thoroughly as they tend to get quite dirty.

Juicing shoots Except for globe artichokes, all of these vegetables can simply be cleaned and juiced as they are. For alfalfa and cress, this will probably mean cutting the shoots from the root as the roots are likely to be embedded in soil. You will need to alternate shoot vegetables with hard vegetables, such as carrots, otherwise no juice will come out.

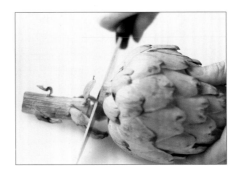

Preparing globe artichokes Remove the woody stem, then cut the rest of the flower into chunks and push through the juicer.

Beans and Mangetout

Choose firm, crisp beans – choices include broad (fava), runner and French (green) beans. Avoid any that have been pre-trimmed or that are going soft. Buying local produce in season is the best option, because out of season beans are usually imported from countries where there might not be any regulations regarding chemical sprays. With the exception of mangetout (snow peas), which make a fairly mild and sweet juice, beans do not taste great when juiced – you will want to mix them with other vegetables.

Therapeutic uses Traditional herbal uses of pod vegetables are as a stimulant for the nervous system, for convalescence, to treat gout and to help support the insulin-producing ability of the pancreas.

Fennel and Celery

These two bulb vegetables make very useful juices. Their tastes are fairly strong so they are best added to other juices, such as carrot, apple or pear, at a ratio of about one-fifth fennel or celery to four-fifths other juice. Fennel tastes of aniseed, and juiced celery, when combined with other juices, does not taste nearly as strong as the raw vegetable. Buy firm, pale green produce for the best flavours.

Therapeutic uses The cleansing actions of these two bulb vegetables are similar, and they are excellent for supporting the liver and gall bladder. Celery also has a strong diuretic action and is often used to calm the nervous system, while fennel is used to manage flatulence and nausea. When combined with carrot juice, fennel is a traditional remedy for failing eyesight. It is also used to ward off headaches and migraines, and some people believe it is helpful in alleviating menstrual and menopausal symptoms.

Onions and Leeks

All onions, including shallots, spring onions (scallions) and even red (Italian) onions, produce strong tasting juices. You only need to add a tiny quantity to a general vegetable juice. Leek juice is not as strong as onion juice but has a similar taste. One of the

Left: Fennel produces a strong aniseed juice that can be overpowering.

problems with onions, as with garlic, is that they can leave a residual taste on the mesh of the machine, meaning that extra cleaning is needed. Running half a lemon through the machine can help to mop up the scent.

Therapeutic uses These bulb vegetables have renowned healing qualities. Onions are recommended for their immune-boosting qualities whenever you have a cold or the flu. They are also antibacterial and antiseptic – leeks have similar but milder actions.

Asparagus

A shoot vegetable, asparagus is available in the spring. It combines well with other vegetables but is not suitable to drink on its own.

Therapeutic uses Asparagus is used as a traditional remedy for kidney problems. The alkaloid asparagine, which is also found in potatoes and beetroot (beet), stimulates the kidneys but also turns urine a dark colour with a distinctive smell. This is not something to worry about, it is simply an indication of its successful diuretic effect.

Left: Leeks are a member of the onion family with similar healing properties.

Beansprouts, Cress and Alfalfa

You can buy beansprouts and cress in most large supermarkets, and alfalfa may be sourced in health food shops. Otherwise you can buy seeds and sprout them yourself (see right). They all give fairly strong tasting, peppery juices, so need to be mixed with other vegetable juices to tone down their flavour. They are probably easier to use in salads than in juices, but some people like to juice them for their distinctive taste.

Therapeutic uses These shoot vegetables have lots of nutritional benefits. Beansprouts are high in many minerals and vitamins, while cress is a member of the brassica family and therefore is believed to provide the same anti-cancer health benefits. Alfalfa has high levels of vitamins A, C and K, but should not be used often because it is high in a compound called canavanine, which is believed to aggravate rheumatoid arthritis.

Below: Beansprouts produce a distinctive, peppery juice.

Below: Mix asparagus juice with other vegetables for the best flavour.

SPROUT YOUR OWN
Leguminous beans, pulses, lentils and peas are not suitable for juicing, but they can be soaked and sprouted and then juiced.

1 Put one type of pulse in a large glass jar. Pour in a generous amount of cold water and leave to soak for 24 hours. Discard the water, rinse the beans under cold running water and drain in a sieve.

2 Put the damp beans back in the jar. Cover with a square of cloth, securing with an elastic band.

3 Leave the beans in a dark, warm place and repeat the rinsing and draining twice a day for 3–4 days.

4 When the beans have sprouted, put them on a windowsill for 24 hours until the shoots turn green. They are now ready for juicing.

Globe Artichoke

The globe artichoke is actually a flower related to the thistle. The heart of the globe and the soft part of the petals attached to the middle are the parts that are normally eaten, but you can juice the whole vegetable, minus any woody parts.

Therapeutic uses The globe artichoke has cleansing and diuretic actions, and is often used to help with liver complaints. It can be used as an effective pick-me-up after festive occasions or parties.

Natural flavourings and health supplements

Herbs and spices have been used for many years for flavouring food, as well as for health and healing purposes. Some of the traditional herbal remedies that have developed over the centuries are now being confirmed as active compounds, and treatments are being refined.

Culinary Herbs

They are so familiar in our everyday cuisine, it is easy to forget that culinary herbs have important health properties. Most fresh herbs go well with vegetable juices; they should be put through a juicer with hard ingredients so the machine does not become clogged up. Alternatively, they can be steeped in the juice, but don't wait too long to drink it or the value of the juice's nutrients will begin to decrease. Fresh herbs can also be finely chopped and added as a garnish. Mint and lemon balm work very well with fruit juices. Lavender flowers, borage and fresh rosemary may also be used in some fruit blends.

Above: If possible, pick fresh mint from your garden for the best flavour.

Basil Fresh basil has a pungent, peppery flavour and a sweet aroma. It is known as a soporific herb because it is very relaxing. Put it through a juicer, followed by a hard vegetable, or crush the leaves using a mortar and pestle. Alternatively, make a tisane with hot water and add this to a juice or blend.

Mint There are many varieties of this prolific herb, which is also a potent digestive aid. Flavours vary but all mints have a strong, sweet aroma and cool aftertaste. Make a tisane and use it to dilute juices.

Left: Basil can either be juiced or used as a tasty garnish.

Right: Dill works well with carrot juice and aids digestion.

Parsley There are two basic varieties of parsley – curly and flat leaf, the latter having the stronger flavour. Use it sparingly. This herb is very rich in a number of nutrients including calcium and betacarotene. It can be put through a juicer, but it must be followed by a hard vegetable, such as carrot.

Chives These are a member of the onion family, and they provide a mild onion flavour. They have the same immune-supporting benefits as all types of onion and leeks.

Rosemary This herb acts as a stimulant to the nervous and circulatory systems and is also thought to relieve indigestion. As an infusion, it is traditionally used to relieve colds and headaches.

Sage Fresh sage has a pungent, slightly bitter aroma. It is an effective alleviator of sweating as a side effect of menopausal hot flushes. Make a tisane with hot water and use to dilute juices. Do not use sage if breastfeeding as it can reduce milk flow.

Dill With its distinctive yet mild caraway-like flavour, dill marries well with all green juices and carrot juice. It is a calming herb and is known to be a soporific. It also aids digestion.

Juniper berries These have antiseptic properties and can be used to treat urinary tract infections such as cystitis. Juniper berries should not be used if you are pregnant or suffer from kidney infections, as they can cause the uterus to contract.

Culinary Spices

As with culinary herbs, these are easy to overlook because they are used in such small quantities in cooking. However, they add wonderful flavourings to many juices and blends and have extremely important therapeutic benefits too.

Horseradish

This pungent root is a potent sinus clearer. Grate a little and add as required to juices but do not put horseradish through a juicer.

Chilli Ranging from fairly mild to fiery hot, it is believed that chilli spices help to build up a strong immune system and may chase off imminent colds and fevers. Use only a tiny amount in vegetable juices and do not put through a juicer or you may end up with chilli-flavoured fruit juices. Grind in a mortar using a pestle, and avoid using the seeds unless you have a very strong constitution.

Above: Remove the seeds from chillies before juicing, unless you are a real fan of hot and spicy blends.

Cumin Strong and nutty, yet slightly bitter, cumin is emerging as one of the most potent antioxidant-rich "super-spices" around. The active compound is curcumin. Dry-roast the seeds, then grind in a mortar using a pestle and add to drinks.

Left: Grate a little horseradish into a juice to add extra spice.

Ginger Fresh or ground ginger is pungent and quite hot. It is a warming spice that naturally lends itself to both fruit and vegetable juices, complementing citrus fruits particularly well. Use the fresh root if you can, otherwise add ground ginger or a supplement.

Above: Root ginger is hot and spicy so use small quantities.

Nutmeg Sweet and aromatic, this is a warming spice, but do not use too much as it can have very unpleasant hallucinogenic effects.

Cardamom These pods can help to relieve vomiting and indigestion. Cardamom sweetens the breath when chewed and is also used to treat colds.

GARLIC

This pungent bulb is regarded as a "super-herb" by juicing fans.

It is a potent blood thinner and immune-system supporter. It is best not to put it through the juicer as you will never get rid of the taste. Instead, pulverize it using a mortar and pestle and add just a tiny bit directly to the juice.

Star anise With a distinct aniseed flavour, star anise is useful for treating inflammation of the respiratory tract, loosening phlegm and calming peptic ulcers. It is also used to treat cramps. Grind the seed and add to a juice.

Cloves The oil from cloves is potent and is traditionally used to numb the gums during dental treatment or to relieve the pain for young children who are teething. Its strong antibacterial properties can be harnessed by making a tisane and adding to drinks, although the flavour of cloves will dominate any other ingredients.

Cinnamon A tree bark, cinnamon helps to soothe unsettled stomachs, can be used to revive your appetite, eases digestive tract spasms and alleviates flatulence. Grind the fresh spice and add half a teaspoon to juices or smoothies – the flavour complements banana, pear and carrot.

Other Useful Herbs, Spices and Supplements

It is easy to add medicinal herbs to blends and juices. Before you do so, however, make sure there are no contra-indications or interactions with any medications you are currently taking – check with your medical practitioner.

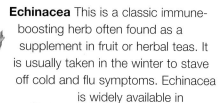

Above: Rosehips are usually made into powder or tablets.

Chamomile This herb has an apple-like scent that belies its pungent, rather bitter flavour. It is a calming herb and is very safe even for children. Use a chamomile teabag, available from larger supermarkets and health food shops, or simply infuse 4–5 fresh flower-heads, then add the infusion to your juice. Chamomile should not be used by anybody who has an allergy to ragwort.

Ginkgo This is excellent for the circulation and is thought to be good for boosting memory. Simply empty a capsule into your blend and mix thoroughly.

Rosehip The reddish-orange fruit of the rose has extremely high levels of vitamin C. Rosehips are usually sold in powdered form or as tablets. Add a small amount of powder to your blend (check the packet for quantities), crumble a tablet in, or make a rosehip tisane and add it to your juice.

Ginseng A sweet liquorice-flavoured root, this is used as an energy booster, and some people even believe it is a libido enhancer. It is also reputed to help with the treatment of high blood pressure. Available in health food shops, simply empty a capsule or sprinkle some of the powder (according to instructions) into your blend.

Milk thistle This is an important liver-supporting herb which marries well with globe artichoke. It can help prevent damage to the liver from alcohol. Empty one or two capsules into your blend.

Liquorice This root has a mild steroid effect and can help relieve the symptoms of most allergies. However, it should not be used alongside steroid medication or by anyone who suffers from high blood pressure as it can cause the retention of sodium and the depletion of potassium. Liquorice is available as a root from most health food shops. Grind the root with a mortar and pestle and sprinkle a little into your blend.

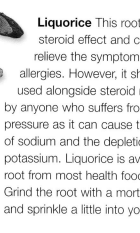

Left: Liquorice can help to relieve allergies.

Echinacea This is a classic immune-boosting herb often found as a supplement in fruit or herbal teas. It is usually taken in the winter to stave off cold and flu symptoms. Echinacea is widely available in tincture form and it is easy to add a few drops to your blend according to instructions, or you could make a tisane with hot water and add this to your drink.

A NATURAL HEALER

Grown from the wholewheat grain, wheatgrass has been recognized for centuries for its general healing qualities. It is a powerful detoxifier and cleanser and a rich source of B vitamins and vitamins A, C and E, as well as all the known minerals. Its vibrant green colour comes from chlorophyll (known as nature's healer), which works directly on the liver to eliminate harmful toxins. Once it is juiced, wheatgrass should be consumed within 15 minutes, preferably on an empty stomach. Wheatgrass juice can be powerful in its effect, and some people may feel dizzy or nauseous the first time they drink it. Sip small amounts until your body gets used to it.

Left: Kelp is a form of seaweed and is packed full of vitamins and minerals.

Other Health Ingredients

Once you realize that supplements can be added to juices, checking for contraindications first, you can become quite adventurous. It is easy to do and beats popping endless vitamin and supplement pills every day.

Brewer's yeast Very rich in B-vitamins and minerals such as iron, zinc, magnesium and potassium, Brewer's yeast also supplies a form of protein. It has a very strong flavour but this becomes a pleasant nutty taste when blended with fruits or vegetables.

Bee pollen This is a useful immune booster and can also help relieve the symptoms of hay fever.

Spirulina and wheatgrass One of the main superjuice ingredients, spirulina is rich in a wide variety of nutrients and vitamins. Both spirulina and wheatgrass are often used as an ingredient in supercharged, healthy juices. They are readily available in powdered form and can easily be added to juices, but you could create your own free supply by growing it at home.

Vitamin C It is extremely easy to add a little vitamin C to your daily juice, whether you use a squeeze of lemon or lime juice, a powder sprinkled into your blend or a tablet crumbled in. A non-acidic version of vitamin C, such as magnesium ascorbate, is gentler on the stomach than most others. Make sure you choose one with bioflavonoids for maximum effect.

Kelp This form of seaweed is naturally very rich in minerals, such as calcium, copper, iron, magnesium, potassium and zinc, B vitamins and betacarotene. It also contains high levels of iodine, which is vital for encouraging the normal functioning of the thyroid gland, but it should not be taken by those with an overactive thyroid. Seaweeds, such as kelp, have long been used to treat those suffering from common colds, constipation, arthritis and rheumatism.

FATS AND OILS

Healthy fats are good sources of essential fatty acids, which can help to clear up a range of complaints including dry skin, listless hair and low energy levels.

Lecithin This is an emulsifier derived from soya, which is ideal to add to a juice or blend before any fats. Add 5–10ml/1–2 tsp to the ingredients in a blender. It tastes pleasant and helps fat digestion.

Evening primrose oil This can be helpful in alleviating pre-menstrual problems and for allergies. Pierce a capsule with a pin and squeeze into your juice or blend.

Walnut oil This oil has a pleasant nutty taste and is light so it does not overwhelm juices. It is a good source of both omega-3 and omega-6 fatty acids, which are useful for nervous and hormonal health. Add 5–10ml/ 1–2 tsp to a glass of juice. Store in the refrigerator.

Sambucol (elderberry extract) During the winter when berries are not readily available or are too expensive, simply add a teaspoonful of sambucol to your juices. This is a rich source of proanthocyanins and will give your immune system a well-deserved boost.

Aloe vera The fleshy succulent plant called aloe vera provides two main products: aloe vera gel, which is used externally for soothing skin irritations and sunburn, and aloe vera juice, which can be added to your juices and blends. Aloe vera juice is reputed to help relieve the symptoms of arthritis, ME and eczema, and is also renowned for soothing and rebuilding the digestive tract. Make sure you choose a certified product with a guaranteed amount of active compounds and add a dose, according to the instructions on the packet, to your blend.

Flax seed oil A "super-oil", this has high levels of omega-3 fatty acids. Add 5–10ml/1–2 tsp to your juice. Store in the refrigerator.

Above: Walnut oil has a nutty flavour that works well in most juices.

Nuts and seeds

These powerhouses of nutrition are excellent sources of protein, fibre, vitamin E, and the minerals zinc, iron, selenium, magnesium and calcium. They also provide the vitamin-like oils called essential fatty acids, which are required for a healthy nervous system, hormone balance and cell structure as well as having potent anti-inflammatory effects which help to control a number of diseases. However, for all their health benefits, some people are allergic to nuts and seeds – peanuts and sesame seeds being the main culprits – so check before offering a blend to someone. Particular care needs to be taken when making drinks for children, who may not be aware that they are allergic.

Below: Pistachio nuts add a delicate green colour to blends, while pecan nuts combine particularly well with banana.

You can use nuts and seeds in juices and blends in a number of ways. They can be ground in a small nut grinder (available separately or as an attachment for food processors). Or you could use a mortar and pestle to grind them. Add them to creamy drinks and juices and mix well. Chopped nuts and seeds also make a pretty decoration when sprinkled on top of smoothies or milkshakes.

Nuts

Choose whole unsalted nuts for making blends and smoothies, and always check the expiry date on packets. After opening a packet of nuts, store any that are left over in a glass jar with a screwtop lid in the refrigerator to keep them fresh. Choose from walnuts, Brazil nuts, pistachio nuts, pecan nuts, hazelnuts or almonds to add flavour and crunch to blended drinks. Peanuts are not really nuts but legumes, a member of the bean family, which is a part of the reason why some people are allergic to them.

You could use various smooth nut butters, which are available from supermarkets or health food shops, to flavour drinks instead of whole nuts. Add them directly to the blend and mix thoroughly. Delicious nut and seed milks, such as almond milk (see right) are easy to make at home and can be used to give smoothies or milkshakes an intense, nutty taste.

Nuts have been shown to have important therapeutic benefits when used to replace other fatty ingredients in the diet. For instance, if you eat walnuts regularly, this can help to reduce the risk of heart disease, while eating peanuts could reduce the risk of contracting diabetes.

MAKING ALMOND MILK
This method can be used for almost any other nuts and seeds as well as almonds.

1 In a heatproof bowl, cover 115g/4oz/1 cup whole almonds with boiling water and leave to stand for 5 minutes. Drain, discarding the water.

2 The skins will now be loose. Squeeze the almonds gently out of their skins.

3 Place the skinned almonds in a blender with 250ml/8fl oz/1 cup water and blend roughly.

4 Add another 250ml/8fl oz/1 cup water and continue blending until you have a thick paste.

5 Gradually add more water until you achieve the consistency you require, somewhere between cream and milk.

6 Blend until no residue remains or strain the almond milk to remove any residue.

Seeds

Buy seeds ready hulled in small packets and keep them as you would nuts. Choose from pumpkin seeds, sunflower seeds, pine nuts, linseeds (flax seeds) and sesame seeds.

Coconut is not really a nut, but a huge seed. It is high in saturated fats so it is best to limit the amount of coconut flesh or milk you use. Linseeds (flax seeds) are particularly rich in an important member of the omega-3 family of fatty acids. The culinary oil derived from linseeds is called flax seed oil. Sesame seeds are made into a thick, rich-tasting purée called tahini, which can be added in small amounts to blended drinks. Dark tahini, which uses the whole seed including the husk, is about ten times richer in calcium than light tahini, and turns it into a calcium-match for milk.

Above: Despite their name, pine nuts are actually a seed.

GRAINS AND FIBRE

When making juices and blends it is easy to sneak in extra healthy ingredients. Grains are excellent sources of B-complex vitamins, vitamin E, calcium, magnesium, iron, zinc and essential fatty acids.

Wheatgerm This comes as a coarse powder and it is easy to add 5ml/1 tsp to a smoothie blend.

Above: Add wheatgerm powder to your blends in small quantities.

Oatmeal Choose fine-ground oatmeal and add 10–15ml/2–3 tsp to a blend, or to milk with some honey for a night-time drink. Oatmeal provides gentle soluble fibre, which is important for reducing cholesterol levels.

Above: Pudding rice works well as a thickener for blended drinks.

Rice Choose rice as a thickener for smoothies or shakes if you are allergic to wheat. Cooked pudding rice works well.

Bran and psyllium Bran is widely available, while psyllium can be bought from health food shops. Oatbran contains soluble fibre, which can help to reduce cholesterol levels. If you suffer from constipation, however, you may be tempted to try wheat bran. Many people with digestive problems find bran too abrasive, so a better option is to add 5–10ml/ 1–2 tsp of psyllium to a blend.

Above: Coconut is delicious but extremely high in saturated fat.

Dairy and dairy alternatives

Adding milk, yogurts, dairy or milk substitutes to blended drinks results in a more luxurious and creamy, though not necessarily more fattening, treat. Milk is calcium-rich (even skimmed milk) and many alternative milks are also now enriched with calcium. You can keep a lid on calorie and fat counts by choosing low-fat versions. Dairy substitutes are useful for people with dairy intolerances, meaning they can still add creamy texture to smoothies and milkshakes.

Milk

For a rich and creamy taste choose full cream (whole) milk. Most people, however, need to avoid too much saturated fat in their diet and would be better advised to use skimmed or semi-skimmed (low-fat) milk.

Therapeutic uses Milk is one of the richest sources of calcium available. Full cream milk is only usually advised for young children, who need the calories it provides to promote growth and bone health.

Below: Yogurt is available in many forms, both low-fat and full-fat. Natural yogurt is ideal, but you could experiment with low-fat flavoured yogurts.

Cream

For extra indulgence, use double (heavy) or single (light) cream, crème fraîche, mascarpone, smetana or, for a different taste, sour cream.

Therapeutic uses Cream is an excellent source of vitamin E, which helps to maintain healthy skin, but it is very high in calories so should be used in moderation.

Yogurt

For making shakes or smoothies thicker, yogurts are an extremely useful ingredient. Greek (US strained plain) yogurt is much thicker than standard varieties but has almost as many calories as cream, so it should not be used on a regular basis. Low-fat yogurts, including low-fat Greek yogurt, are readily available instead, so you can still indulge yourself without feeling too guilty. Fruit yogurts can add interesting flavours to fruity blends.

Therapeutic uses Yogurt is rich in calcium and it is often suitable even for people who have a milk intolerance. Choosing live "bio" yogurt can help improve digestive tract health by providing healthy bacteria. High-fibre yogurts that have cholesterol-lowering properties are now available.

Above: Many low-fat alternative milks are now calcium-enriched.

ALTERNATIVE MILKS

Often used by people who have a dairy allergy, alternative milks are a good low-calorie option. The fats in most nut milks, except for coconut, are healthy polyunsaturated fats.

Soya milk Choose the calcium-enriched variety of soya milk if you are using it instead of cow's milk on a regular basis.

Rice milk This has a thinner and lighter consistency than cow's milk, but a deliciously sweet flavour. Vanilla- and chocolate-flavoured rice milks are also available.

Oat milk This alternative to cow's milk is extremely rich and has a creamy, smooth taste.

Nut milks Coconut milk is delicious but, because it has a very rich flavour, it is best if you either dilute it or use just a small amount. You can now buy almond milk and various other nut milks from most large supermarkets or health food shops.

Above: Use real strawberry ice cream to make a traditional milkshake.

Frozen Ingredients

Ice creams, sorbets (sherbets), frozen yogurts and soya ices can all be scooped straight from the freezer to make a delicious old-fashioned shake.

Therapeutic uses Dairy ice cream is a good source of calcium, although it is high in calories, but non-dairy ice creams and sorbets do not have the benefit of calcium.

Low-fat Creamy Ingredients

Fromage frais (cream cheese) and plain cottage cheese can both be bought in low-fat versions and used as creamy thickeners, as can buttermilk which is slightly sour tasting.

Therapeutic uses These are perfect for anybody on a calorie-controlled diet.

Tofu

Also known as soya bean curd and beancurd, tofu is available in three different textures: firm, medium-firm and silken. Naturally a fairly bland food with a slight nutty taste, it will affect the texture of drinks, but not the taste. Soft, silken tofu has the best texture for blending and adds a creamy thickness to the blend.

Therapeutic uses Tofu is an all-round healthy food – high in protein, low in saturated fats and calories, easy to digest and cholesterol-free. It has high levels of calcium and lots of vitamin E, which is important for maintaining healthy skin and helps protect against heart disease.

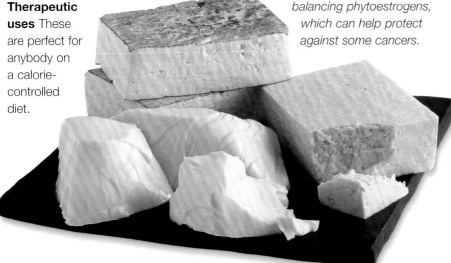

Below: Tofu is rich in hormone-balancing phytoestrogens, which can help protect against some cancers.

EGGS

Raw eggs contain high levels of vitamin B12, which is vital for the nervous system. Eggs are often used as the basis of protein shakes by sports enthusiasts or in hangover remedies to kick-start the system. Before using raw eggs in a blend, you should be aware of the following:

• Raw egg white binds with the B-vitamin biotin and, if overused, can lead to a deficiency of this nutrient.
• Pregnant women, children, the sick or elderly, or those with an impaired immune system should not consume raw eggs, because of the risk of salmonella. (While chickens are often routinely vaccinated for salmonella in some countries, there is still a residual risk from unvaccinated flocks.)
• Eggs have a high cholesterol content, contained in the yolk. People who have high cholesterol levels may benefit from limiting their egg intake to five a week. However, as we make most of the cholesterol in the body (cholesterol is needed for cell maintenance) and this is adversely affected by a high saturated fat intake, it is more beneficial to reduce saturated fats from butter, cheese and meat.
• Eggs that have been produced to contain high levels of omega-3 fatty acids are now widely available and these could make an important contribution to heart health.

Above: Raw eggs can thicken blends nicely but it is not safe for everybody to eat them.

Sweeteners and other flavourings

We are all naturally attracted to sweet-tasting foods. The advantage of juices and smoothies is that it is possible to give in to that craving occasionally, with some indulgent additions, and yet still know that you are benefiting from the healthy basic ingredients.

Many juices, whether made from fruit or vegetables, are naturally sweet, so you may find that you need to dilute them slightly to reduce their sweetness. This can easily be done by adding one-third to one-half water – either still or sparkling, according to taste. You could also add a variety of milky ingredients. Adding water or milk will ensure that blood sugar levels rise more slowly. Children should always drink juices that are diluted to reduce the impact on their teeth.

If a juice, smoothie or milkshake is not sweet enough, you could simply add some sugar – white, brown or muscovado (molasses) – or flavoured syrups, such as vanilla, or fruit cordials. There are, however, many other sweeteners that can be used.

Honey

Different honeys have varying tastes, depending on which type of pollen the bees have gathered. Popular choices are lavender or apple blossom honey, which have a fragrant sweetness. Manuka honey is renowned for its health-promoting properties; it is anti-bacterial, making it ideal for sore throats. Honey should not be fed to children under the age of 12 months as it could cause botulism, a type of food poisoning that can be fatal.

Fructose

Instead of using table sugar (sucrose) you could use fructose (a totally natural fruit sugar). This has a lower Glycaemic Index (GI) score than sucrose so can be used in moderation by diabetics. (The GI is a measure of how fast a carbohydrate enters the blood stream as sugar. The higher the score, the less healthy the carbohydrate.) Fructose is sweeter than table sugar so do not use as a direct substitution in drinks.

Above: Blackstrap molasses is intensely sweet and so only a tiny bit is needed.

Blackstrap Molasses

During the refining of sugar, the juice squeezed from the cane or beet is boiled until syrupy and then the sugar crystals are extracted. There are three boilings, resulting in light molasses, then dark and finally blackstrap molasses, which is thick, dark and rather bitter. It is a rich source of calcium, iron and magnesium but only a little should be used.

Above: Choose from many different flavours and types of honey.

Above: Liven up parties by adding a few shots of alcohol to your punchbowl.

Above: Try crumbling brownies on top of your favourite chocolate milkshake.

Above: When added to your blends, meringues give an irresistible crunch.

FOS (fructooligosaccharide)

This is a natural fibre found in bananas, Jerusalem artichokes, tomatoes, onions and many other fruits and vegetables. It looks like sugar and is almost as sweet but it has no effect on blood sugar levels. It can be found in health food shops. Using a moderate amount has a beneficial effect on digestive tract health as it promotes the growth of good bacteria, but too much FOS can lead to bloating.

Other Flavourings

Many other ingredients and sweet additions can be included in smoothies. Health-promoting properties become less important here – everyone deserves to indulge themselves occasionally.

Coffee Freshly ground or instant, coffee is just the thing if you need a wake-up call with your morning blend. Try adding it to creamy blends to make a coffee-flavoured smoothie or shake. Use decaffeinated coffee if you are caffeine sensitive and, if you are feeling particularly virtuous, try using dandelion coffee, which is reputed to have liver-cleansing properties.

Chocolate This is an irresistible ingredient, whether melted, grated or in powder form. Dark (bittersweet) chocolate is the best for you as it is rich in iron and antioxidants, but for a milder flavour you should use milk chocolate. For a decadent finish, grate or shave chocolate on top of your smoothie – dark, plain (semisweet), milk or white, whichever you prefer.

Sweets (candies) Try adding sweets to the side of the glass as a decoration that is guaranteed to impress at a kid's party, or add them to the blender and blend them into the drink. Turkish delight or nougat are good choices, or you could serve a smoothie with an edible swizzle stick in the shape of a chocolate wand.

Cakes and cookies Brownies or meringues can be crumbled on top of smoothies or added to the blend for texture, and any other cakes or cookies can be used instead if they complement the drink you are serving. Amaretti provide a lovely almond accent, for example, which would be delicious with strawberry, apricot or peach-based blends, or try crunchy coconut macaroons sprinkled on top of a tropical fruit blend.

Alcohol Add a splash of alcohol to your favourite drinks when you just want to relax with a smoothie at the end of the day, or give your party juices a boost. Choose different drinks for their flavours, such as coffee, mint or orange liqueurs, or give your blend a real kick by adding a shot (or two) of brandy or whisky.

Above: Create a traditional, decadent milkshake with rich, dark chocolate.

54

Juicing and blending in a healthy diet

Following a healthy diet is one of the most fundamental ways in which you can ensure optimal energy levels, balanced moods, a zest for life and, of course, good general health. For overall wellbeing, it is also important to take sufficient exercise and to maintain a positive attitude to life.

What constitutes a healthy diet? Fresh fruit and vegetables are the most essential aspect – at least five portions a day – and drinking juices will keep you rehydrated as well as ensuring that you get the recommended amounts. These four easy-to-follow rules could help you develop a regime that will set you up for life.

1 Eat a wide variety of fresh foods to make sure you get all the vitamins and minerals you need.
2 Base your diet on fruits, vegetables, grains, legumes, nuts, seeds and eggs. If you are a meat-eater, always select lean cuts and restrict your intake of red meats. Fresh, unprocessed fish is always a healthier option.
3 Keep processed, salty, sugary or fatty foods to a minimum.
4 Drink sufficient water to stay hydrated: 1.5–2 litres/2½–4 pints/1½–2 quarts per day is the usual recommendation.

Above: Cantaloupe melons are high in betacarotene and support the immune system.

Therapeutic Juicing

In order to receive the therapeutic benefits from juices, you will need to incorporate the suggested juice on a regular basis – daily, if possible. However, remember that therapeutic juicing is not intended to take the place of eating balanced, healthy meals, but should always be an addition to your health routine.

Juices have been used by herbalists, naturopaths and nutritionists for centuries to prevent illness and alleviate ailments. However, self-diagnosis and treatment of any serious condition is not really advisable, and you should always check with your health practitioner if any symptoms persist.

Their acidity and sugar levels mean that juices can have an eroding effect on teeth. To minimize this, it is best to consume them alongside meals. You can also reduce the effect by adding milk and dairy substitutes, which are more alkaline and so temper the acidic effect – calcium-rich choices are also tooth-friendly. Avoid brushing your teeth for an hour after drinking a juice as the enamel on the teeth needs time to harden again.

Immune System Health and Allergies

Antioxidants found in fruits and vegetables are extremely important in supporting the immune system. There are a number of fruits and vegetables that are particularly helpful in this respect. Foods that are rich in betacarotene, such as carrots and cantaloupe melons, and dark red or blue fruits, such as cherries and blueberries, are very supportive of the

THE POWER OF ANTIOXIDANTS
Antioxidants protect you against a number of diseases which are caused by free radicals. The plants actually make these antioxidants to protect themselves but when we eat those plants, we enjoy the benefits. Free radicals are largely a by-product of oxidization, such as when iron rusts or a cut apple turns brown. In humans this damage results in cataracts, inflammation, damage to blood vessels and cancer. Vitamins A, C and E are antioxidants but there are also thousands of phytonutrients, which are highly protective as well. Only plant foods give us these valuable nutrients and juicing is a way of ensuring that you give yourself a good level of protection.

immune system. Foods rich in vitamin C, such as blackcurrants and kiwi fruit, are also important. Additionally, specific compounds, such as resveratrol in grapes and lycopene in watermelons and tomatoes, are thought to help keep the immune system healthy.

The brassica family, which includes broccoli, cabbage, Brussels sprouts and cauliflower, are thought to be potent cancer fighters. Garlic, onions and leeks are all good weapons for fighting off colds, coughs and flu. If you find raw onion or garlic in juice a little too strong, try a delicious warm onion and garlic broth instead. Quince was traditionally used to help people through periods of convalescence, and it is still recommended by many people today.

Anyone with allergies, unless they are allergic to a particular fruit or vegetable, will benefit from at least five portions daily to strengthen their immune system and raise the threshold at which allergic reactions are triggered. Dark red and purple berries seem to be particularly effective in this respect.

Right:
Quercitin,
found in onions,
is good for the lungs.

Respiratory Health

The delicate tissues of the respiratory tract can be strengthened and supported by using particular fruits and vegetables. Quercitin, which is found in apples and onions, has a strengthening effect on the lungs, and dark red and purple berries have potent lung supporting properties, which result from the high levels of proanthocyanins they contain.

Catarrh can often be reduced by avoiding dairy products, while the inclusion of garlic in juices and blends – and in your diet generally – will also help to reduce the build up of catarrh. Turnips have expectorant properties, and radish and horseradish, used in very small amounts, can also help to clear the sinuses.

People who suffer badly from hay fever may find that nettles are useful in helping to alleviate their symptoms.

Cleansing and Urinary Tract Health

Keeping the body cleansed of toxins is an obvious way to maintain good health. General detoxing effects can be helped along by juicing fruits that are naturally high in pectin and/or ellagic acid, such as apples, strawberries and grapes.

Liver-supporting ingredients include globe artichoke, lemon and cranberry. Fennel juice helps to detoxify the liver,

and is also useful in helping to restore a general feeling of wellbeing. Radish helps to support the gall bladder, which is where bile is stored before being discharged into the duodenum, where it aids the emulsification and absorption of fats.

Juices that have a diuretic action, reducing water retention and stimulating the kidneys, include celery, cucumber, cranberry, dandelion, celeriac, fennel, strawberry, peach and watermelon. In the last case, leave the pips (seeds) in for extra potassium when juicing and throw in a piece of the rind for some extra nutrients. Asparagine, found in asparagus, also stimulates the kidneys and helps to purify the blood. It makes the urine turn a dark colour, with a distinctive smell, but this is not harmful and is actually an indication that it is doing its job properly.

If you suffer from cystitis or other urinary infections, drink plenty of fresh cranberry or blueberry juice. These juices are known to help prevent bacteria from adhering to the urinary tract. Garlic is also a potent antibacterial ingredient and may be useful in treating this unpleasant and painful condition.

Digestive Health

A healthy digestive system is vital for optimal health and to ensure the maximum absorption of nutrients from foods. For both constipation and diarrhoea, add 5–10ml/1–2 tsp ground linseeds (flax seeds) or 5ml/1 tsp psyllium husks to a drink daily. Laxative effects can also be induced with plums, prunes, peaches, nectarines, figs or pears. Ginger is a traditional remedy for nausea, including morning sickness in early pregnancy.

Apples are high in pectin, malic acid and tannic acid, all of which help to normalize digestive function (and improve liver function). Fennel juice is excellent for most digestive conditions,

Above: Cranberry juice can help to relieve urinary tract infections.

Below: Apples are useful for aiding digestion and cleansing the liver.

Below: Cucumbers are full of the valuable mineral potassium.

while indigestion, impaired digestion and stomach ulcers respond well to pineapples or papayas. Cabbagin, a compound in cabbages, helps to heal the gut wall and, along with potato juice, is a useful remedy for ulcers. All fruits and vegetables are good sources of fibre, which helps to keep the bowels in good general health. Drinking smoothies rather than juices will increase your fibre intake, as the fibrous, pulpy part of the fruit is preserved in the drink.

Circulation and Blood Health

A healthy blood supply will deliver oxygen, the primary nutrient, to all of your cells. For general circulation and blood health, including arterial health, be sure to eat plenty of dark green leafy vegetables. These are rich in folic acid, which helps to lower levels of homocysteine, a substance that may be a contributor to osteoporosis. The bioflavonoids in citrus fruits, known as rutin and hesperidin, also support healthy blood vessels and so help to prevent varicose veins.

Raw beetroot (beet) and dandelion juices, along with dark green leafy vegetables, are traditionally used to combat anaemia, and if you combine these with citrus juice or tomato juice, this will serve to improve iron absorption. Potassium, which is found at fairly high levels in all fruit and vegetables, helps to lower blood pressure – watermelon, cucumber, grapes and bananas are especially good sources.

Reproductive and Sexual Health

The health of the next generation depends upon healthy parents. It is now recognized that both parents should ensure that they are in optimum health before conception. This can cause problems, because many women do not realize they are pregnant until a number of weeks after they have conceived, yet the very early stages of pregnancy are the most important for the development of a healthy baby.

For men, zinc is essential for healthy sperm and can be found in nuts and seeds. For women, folic acid is vital preconceptually and in the first trimester. It is used to help form the baby's cells, and there is now a proven link between folic acid deficiency and the incidence of neural tube defects in babies, such as spina bifida. Folic acid can be found in green leafy vegetables and in citrus fruit.

For older generations, a flagging libido may be revitalized by adding warming ginger and ginseng to juices or blends. Women with perimenopausal symptoms can try adding 50–90g/2–3½oz silken tofu or 300ml/½ pint/1¼ cups soya milk to drinks on a daily basis for their valuable phytoestrogens, as these mimic the action of the female hormone oestrogen.

Skeletal and Muscular Health

Looking after your bones is most important in your youth, when you build up maximum density, and in old age, when this density is declining. Weight-bearing exercise is extremely helpful in maintaining healthy bones.

Magnesium-rich foods are needed to help calcium utilization in bones – these include all types of green leafy vegetables, nuts and seeds. They are also good for alleviating muscular cramps, including menstrual cramps. Magnesium-rich juices or blends, taken on a daily basis, will help to improve bone health considerably.

Cucumber juice helps combat rheumatoid arthritis and many other juices are also useful in this respect, including cherry, grape, pineapple and dandelion. Rheumatic pain may be eased by adding some elderberry juice.

Milk, yogurt or calcium-enriched alternative milks added to blends or smoothies is an easy and delicious way to make sure you get enough calcium in your diet. Vitamin D, which is made in the skin, is vital for calcium use by bones and the best source is half an hour of sunlight exposure each day during spring and summer – although this is not always possible in some climates. If you are convalescing or susceptible to osteoporosis, add the contents of a vitamin D supplement to a juice every day.

Above: Seeds are rich in magnesium, which helps maintain healthy bones.

Above: Juice seedless black grapes when you want to unwind.

General Health

Juices help to bring a healthy glow to your skin, a sparkle to your eyes and a glossy sheen to your hair, as well as putting a spring in your step.

Fruit and vegetables that are rich in vitamin C, such as citrus fruits, strawberries, blackcurrants, green (bell) peppers and cabbage, help to build collagen for general skin health, so add these to your juices regularly. A healthy intake of vitamin C has also been proven to prevent the damage that leads to cataracts forming in the lens of the eye. To help alleviate the symptoms of eczema, try adding a tablespoon of flax seed oil to your blends each day – you can help to emulsify it into the blend by adding a teaspoon of lecithin.

Eyes need betacarotene to maintain good health, and this antioxidant can be derived in large quantities from such ingredients as blueberries and spinach. Watercress is rich in sulphur, which helps with the healthy growth of hair and nails, while cucumbers and courgettes (zucchini) are also great for healthy nails.

Grapes have long been used as a traditional rest-cure, but if you want to boost your energy levels, pears, bananas, yams and sweet potatoes are all good choices to add to your blends – try them first thing in the morning to kick-start your system. Betacarotene-rich fruit and vegetables, such as apricots, carrots, cantaloupe melons, red peppers, squashes and spinach help to protect the skin against sun damage.

If you are on a calorie-controlled diet to aid weight loss, this can be speeded up by including filling, nutrient-rich, but low calorie juices based on fruits and vegetables. Drinking juices should help prevent you snacking through-out the day. Use fat-free dairy products instead of half-fat or full-fat ones – you will still get the same amount of calcium from these. However, if blood-sugar swings are a problem for you, dilute your juices or blends by half with water, always drink them with meals and sip slowly.

Mental and Nervous Health

A balanced mood depends, in part, on a balanced diet. The saying "You are what you eat" is equally applicable to mental health as it is to physical health.

If you are feeling lethargic, turnip and dandelion are traditional nerve tonics, while beans also stimulate the nervous system. On the other hand, if you are feeling tense, celery can have a truly restful effect, while lettuce juice has a sedative action and helps to promote sleep. Oatmeal is another traditional calming remedy.

Lavender is thought to reduce headaches; try making a tisane with a few lavender spikes and adding it to a juice. Fennel is also a traditional remedy for headaches and migraines. Nervous eczema can be a recurrent problem for some people when they're not feeling 100 per cent. This can sometimes be relieved with small quantities of potato juice. Memory and moods are helped by a good intake of B-vitamins, which are found in

wheatgerm, brewer's yeast, yogurt, vegetable extract, molasses, peanut butter, oranges and other citrus fruits, sweet potatoes and broccoli.

Anti-stress nutrients that help to support the adrenal glands, which produce stress hormones, are magnesium, found in green leafy vegetables, nuts and seeds, B-vitamins and vitamin C, found in blackcurrants, citrus fruit, strawberries, Brussels sprouts and peppers.

SYNDROME X

This is the term for a condition that could also be described as pre-diabetes, when cells become resistant to the effects of insulin. Insulin is produced by the body in response to the sugar and carbohydrates in your diet. If you tend to suffer from sugar and carbohydrate cravings, tiredness, difficulty concentrating (especially mid-afternoon), and have problems controlling your weight, then you could be suffering from difficulty in managing your blood-sugar levels. If this is the case, make sure that you dilute juices with water by half and sip them slowly instead of drinking them down in one go. Alternatively, add milk, yogurt or soya milk to the mix to slow down the effect on blood sugar.

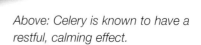

Above: Celery is known to have a restful, calming effect.

Vitamins and minerals

These nutrients are needed in the diet in tiny amounts, but they are essential for health. It has been established that many people do not get their recommended daily allowances (RDAs) of many of these nutrients. Drinking fresh juices and blends made from fruits and vegetables naturally boosts the quantity of vitamins and minerals that you intake daily.

VITAMINS
Vitamin A – Retinol

This vitamin is needed for healthy eyes, skin and mucus membranes (lungs, digestive tract and immune system). Retinol is available only from animal sources such as full cream (whole) dairy produce, oily fish, egg yolks and liver. Large amounts of vitamin A in the diet can be toxic. Betacarotene converts to vitamin A only as it is needed, and so is non-toxic.

Juicing It Betacarotene is found in orange-coloured fruit and vegetables. It is also present in dark green, leafy vegetables. As vitamin A needs fat for absorption, conversion and use, adding a little flax seed oil or similar to betacarotene-rich juices will help.

Vitamin B1 – Thiamine

This is needed to produce energy and to support the nervous system. It is mainly found in cereals and wholegrains, but other non-juicing sources include legumes and meat.

Juicing It Cauliflower, pineapple, orange, leek, brewer's yeast and peanuts are all good sources of vitamin B_1.

Vitamin B2 – Riboflavin

Also needed for energy production, it supports the growth of healthy skin, hair and nails. It is mainly supplied by cereals and wholegrains, but other non-juicing sources are fish and liver.

Juicing It Try juicing broccoli, apricots, spinach and watercress for plenty of vitamin B_2, or add small amounts of brewer's yeast to juices and blends. Milk, yogurt and cottage cheese are also very good sources, and these can be used in smoothies.

Vitamin B3 – Niacin

Niacin is needed for energy production and it helps promote a feeling of calm. Mainly found in fortified cereals, the niacin equivalent, tryptophan, is also in meat, milk and eggs.

Juicing It Juice potatoes, beansprouts, strawberries, parsley, (bell) peppers, avocados, figs and dates. Add wheatgerm to juices and blends.

Vitamin B5 – Pantothenic Acid

Needed for energy production and to control the effects of stress, this vitamin is widely available.

Juicing It Broccoli, berries, watermelon, celery and sweet potatoes all provide pantothenic acid, as well as wheatgerm, brewer's yeast, vegetable extract, molasses and nuts.

Vitamin B6 – Pyridoxine

Needed for processing protein, vitamin B_6 is also used for supporting the nervous and immune systems, and is necessary for healthy skin. It is found in fish, meat, poultry, eggs and wholegrains.

Juicing It Oranges, brassicas, bananas, potatoes and yam provide pyridoxine. Also add watermelon and pumpkin seeds or wheatgerm to drinks.

Vitamin B12 – Cobalamine

Needed to metabolize iron and for a healthy nervous system, this vitamin is found in animal sources or yeast.

Juicing It Vegetable extract is a good source, and can be added to tomato or other vegetable juices. Milk, yogurt and cottage cheese, used in smoothies, provide some vitamin B_{12}.

Folic Acid

This is essential preconceptually and in early pregnancy for healthy foetal development. It works best when combined with vitamins B_{12} and B_6. Fortified cereals are an excellent source.

Juicing It Citrus fruits, broccoli, Brussels sprouts, lettuce, potato, beetroot (beet), apricots, pumpkin, peanuts and almonds are all valuable sources.

Above: Broccoli juice is packed with essential minerals and vitamins.

Vitamin C – Ascorbic Acid

This vitamin supports immunity and bone health. It is needed for skin repair and aids recuperation. It also helps in the absorption of iron, and protects against heart disease and cancer.

Juicing It Raspberries, strawberries, blackcurrants, citrus fruits, papaya and kiwi fruit are good sources of vitamin C. Also try adding beetroot (beet), tomatoes, (bell) peppers, cabbage, cauliflower, watercress and potatoes to juices and smoothies.

Vitamin D

Vital in helping calcium build healthy bones and teeth, vitamin D also protects against breast and prostate cancer. It is mainly made by the skin on exposure to the sun. Half an hour per day is needed on the face, hands and arms during sunny months. The most useful dietary source is oily fish, such as mackerel and salmon, and vitamin D is also added to margarines.

Juicing It There are no food sources of vitamin D to add to juices. Vitamin drops can help to make up a shortfall, but follow the manufacturer's instructions as an excess can be toxic.

Vitamin E

This antioxidant protects against heart disease and ageing, and it also thins the blood. Wholegrains are a valuable source.
Juicing It Vitamin E is found in all nuts and seeds and their oils (it is there to protect them from going rancid). Other sources include dark green leafy vegetables, cream and wheatgerm.

Vitamin K

This is essential for healthy blood clotting and wound repair, and is also needed to maintain healthy bones.
Juicing It Leafy vegetables are a good source of vitamin K, but cauliflower is the richest source. Yogurt supports healthy gut flora, which make vitamin K.

MINERALS
Calcium

Essential for healthy bones, calcium is also important for muscle and heart health and blood clotting. Non-juicing sources include canned fish with bones (sardines and salmon) and wholegrains.
Juicing It Good juicing sources include green leafy vegetables, broccoli and cabbage. Kale contains as much calcium as milk. It is also found in dairy produce (but not butter or cream) and in calcium-fortified dairy substitutes, such as soya milk or rice milk, as well as tofu.

Chromium

This mineral is used in glucose-tolerance factor, a dietary compound that is used for regulating blood sugar levels. Shellfish, mushrooms and chicken are non-juicing sources.
Juicing It Carrots, cabbage, lettuce, oranges, apples and bananas are all good sources, and chromium is also found in milk.

Iodine

This is needed for thyroid health, metabolism, energy and mental function. Non-juicing sources include fish, white rice and iodized salt.
Juicing It Vegetables contain iodine, but only if they have been grown in iodine-rich soil. Seaweed (kelp) is a good source and milk also contains some iodine.

Iron

Needed to make blood and deliver oxygen to cells, iron deficiency can result in lethargy and slowed mental function. Meat is the source of the most easily absorbed form of iron. Vegetarian protein substitutes, such as beans and lentils, are also important sources.
Juicing It Dark green leafy vegetables and dried fruit are good juicing sources. Nuts and seeds, molasses and dark (bittersweet) chocolate can also provide extra iron. Uptake of iron from plant sources is doubled when taken with juices that contain plenty of vitamin C.

Magnesium

Needed for healthy bones, magnesium works in synergy with calcium.
Juicing It Juicing sources include green leafy vegetables, potatoes, citrus fruits and dried fruit. Nuts and seeds also contain magnesium.

Manganese

Involved in the metabolism of fats and carbohydrates, non-juicing sources are eggs and wholegrain cereals.
Juicing It Juice green leafy vegetables, peas and beetroot (beet) for manganese. Add nuts to blends and smoothies.

Phosphorus

Important for bones and teeth, as well as for kidney health.
Juicing It Celery, broccoli, melon, grapes, kiwi fruit and blackcurrants are all good juicing sources, as well as milk.

Potassium

This mineral is needed for healthy nerves, brain health and good kidney function. It counterbalances sodium from salt and helps to lower blood pressure.
Juicing It Juicing sources include all fruit and vegetables.

Selenium

This has antioxidant properties and is good for liver and cardiovascular health. Sources include fish, wholegrains and rice.
Juicing It Brazil nuts are the richest source, along with green vegetables, garlic, onions, tomatoes and wheatgerm.

Sodium

This is needed for healthy nerve function. However, we get too much of the sodium in our diet from salt, which contributes to high blood pressure and heart disease.
Juicing It Sodium is present in small quantities in all fruit and vegetables and is balanced by potassium and water. Seaweeds are alternative sources.

Sulphur

This mineral is needed to maintain healthy skin, hair and nails.
Juicing It Good juicing sources are cabbage, garlic, onion, radish, cucumber, watercress, grapes and berries.

Zinc

Involved in all protein metabolism, zinc is very important for growth and healing, reproduction, immunity and digestion. Meat and fish are the richest sources available, but other non-juicing sources include vegetarian proteins, such as beans and pulses. Zinc is also found in brown rice and wholegrains.
Juicing It Broccoli, cauliflower, carrots, cucumbers and raspberries are the best juicing sources of zinc. Also, try adding nuts and seeds, wheatgerm and brewer's yeast to drinks, as these are also good sources.

Below: Drinks made from grapes and berries provide sulphur for healthy skin.

the recipes

Whether you fancy a creamy, indulgent smoothie,
a healthy vegetable juice, a fruity, aromatic blend
or a refreshing alcoholic punch, you'll find the
perfect recipe here.

super
healthy
juices

This chapter contains a selection of fabulous
juices that have wonderful health benefits.
Highly nutritious, natural additives such as
wheatgrass, sprouting beans, echinacea and kelp
are combined with everyday fruit and vegetables
to make a range of feel-good juices for the
seriously health-conscious.

Parsnip pep

Although parsnips yield a relatively small amount of juice, the juicer produces an amazingly thick, sweet and creamy drink, perfect for adding body to any raw fruit and vegetable blend. Refreshing fennel, apple and pear are the perfect foils for the intense sweetness of parsnip and together produce the most tantalizing power-pack of a fresh juice.

Makes 2 glasses

115g/4oz fennel
200g/7oz parsnips
1 apple
1 pear
a small handful of flat leaf parsley
crushed ice

Cook's tip
Parsnips are at their sweetest a few weeks after the first frost, so try a shot of this wonderful juice when you are most in need of a little winter boost.

1 Using a sharp knife, cut the fennel and parsnips into large similar-sized chunks. Quarter the apple and pear, carefully removing the core, if you like, then cut the quartered pieces in half.

2 Push half the prepared fruit and vegetables through a juicer, then follow with the parsley and the remaining fruit and vegetables.

3 Fill short glasses with ice and pour the juice over. Serve immediately.

Clean sweep

This juice is so packed with goodness, you can almost feel it cleansing and detoxing your body. As well as valuable vitamins, the carrots and grapes provide plenty of natural sweetness, which blends perfectly with the mild pepperiness of the celery and fresh scent of parsley. Drink this juice on a regular basis to give your system a thorough clean-out.

Makes 1 large or 2 small glasses

1 celery stick
300g/11oz carrots
150g/5oz green grapes
several large sprigs of parsley
celery or carrot sticks, to serve

2 Pour into one or two glasses and serve with celery or carrot stick stirrers.

Cook's tip
When juicing herbs, do not remove their individual stalks because it is the stalks that contain all the goodness and flavour – and they go through the juicing machine really easily. Parsley contains calcium, vitamins and iron and also works as a natural cleanser and breath freshener.

1 Using a sharp knife, roughly chop the celery and carrots. Push half of the celery, carrots and grapes through a juicer, then add the parsley sprigs. Add the remaining celery, carrots and grapes in the same way and juice until thoroughly combined.

Bean-good

Beansprouts are a highly nutritious food, bursting with vitamins B and C, and they are one of the few vegetables that actually increase in goodness after they are picked. Although mild in flavour, their juiciness works well in any nourishing blend. Mixed with broccoli, another superfood, and naturally sweet fruits, this blend is a real tonic for your skin, hair and general health.

Makes 1 large or 2 small glasses

90g/3½oz broccoli
1 large pear
90g/3½oz/scant ½ cup beansprouts
200g/7oz green grapes
ice cubes and sliced green grapes

3 Push all the ingredients through the juicer. Pour into glasses and serve with ice cubes and sliced green grapes.

Cook's tip
When juicing fruits and vegetables, always use the freshest ingredients you can find; that way the juice will have maximum flavour and you'll get additional health benefits. If at all possible, use organic produce. This is a bit more expensive but is definitely worth it – you can really taste the difference and your body will reap the rewards.

1 Using a small, sharp knife cut the broccoli into pieces small enough to fit through a juicer funnel.

2 Quarter the pear and carefully remove the core, then roughly chop the flesh into small chunks.

Wheatgrass tonic

The nutritional benefits of wheatgrass are enormous. It is grown from wheat berries and is a concentrated source of chlorophyll, which combats tiredness and fatigue, and also provides enzymes, vitamins and minerals. It has a distinctive flavour so in this juice it is blended with mild white cabbage, but it is just as tasty combined with other vegetables instead.

Makes 1 small glass

50g/2oz white cabbage
90g/3½oz wheatgrass

1 Using a small, sharp knife, roughly shred the cabbage.

2 Push through a juicer with the wheatgrass. Pour the juice into a small glass and serve immediately.

Immune zoom

Red- and orange-coloured fruits and vegetables are particularly good for protecting against or fighting off colds or flu, and are full of powerful antioxidants that are known to protect against many more serious illnesses. This refreshing, fruity drink also contains a herbal blend called echinacea, which helps to relieve the symptoms of colds and flu.

Makes 2 glasses

1 small mango
1 eating apple
2 passion fruit
juice of 1 orange
5ml/1 tsp echinacea
mineral water (optional)
ice cubes (optional)

Cook's tip
If you are suffering from a cold or flu, or can sense its imminent arrival, echinacea can be taken in about 5ml/1 tsp servings, which can be repeated throughout the day. Check the recommended dosage on the manufacturer's packaging before use, however.

1 Halve the mango, cutting down one side of the flat stone (pit). Remove the stone and scoop the flesh from the skin. Roughly chop the flesh and place in a blender or food processor.

2 Peel, core and roughly chop the apple. Add to the blender and process together until smooth, scraping the mixture down from the side of the bowl, if necessary.

3 Halve the passion fruit and scoop the pulp into the mango and apple purée. Add the orange juice and echinacea, then blend briefly.

4 Thin with a little mineral water, if you like, pour into two glasses and serve. Otherwise, transfer the juice into a jug (pitcher) and chill in the refrigerator, then serve in large glasses with ice cubes and slices of mango to decorate.

Ginseng juice

This vibrantly coloured, deliciously tangy juice is also an excellent boost for the immune system. Ginseng is a natural cure-all that is claimed to stimulate digestion, reduce tiredness, alleviate stress, strengthen the immune system and even revive a flagging libido. Here it is added to the juice as a powder but it can also be taken as a dietary supplement in tablet form.

Makes 1 glass

1 red or orange (bell) pepper
200g/7oz pumpkin
1 large apricot
squeeze of lemon juice
5ml/1 tsp ginseng powder
ice cubes

Cook's tip
When seeding peppers, halve them, then cut around the stalk. Give the stalk a sharp pull and the core will come away easily.

1 Using a sharp knife, discard the core from the pepper and roughly chop the flesh. Slice the pumpkin in half. Scoop out the pips (seeds) with a spoon and then cut away the skin. Chop the flesh. Halve and stone (pit) the apricot.

2 Push the pumpkin, pepper and apricot pieces through a juicer. Add a squeeze of lemon juice and the ginseng powder, and stir well to mix together. Pour the juice over ice cubes in a tall glass and serve.

Red alert

This juice is perfect for those times when you're not thinking straight or you need to concentrate. Beetroot, carrots and spinach all contain folic acid, which is known to help maintain a healthy brain, while the addition of fresh orange juice will give your body a natural vitamin boost. This delicious and vibrant blend is guaranteed to set your tastebuds tingling.

Makes 1 large or 2 small glasses

200g/7oz raw beetroot (beets)
1 carrot
1 large orange
50g/2oz spinach

1 Using a sharp knife, cut the beetroot into wedges. Roughly chop the carrot, then cut away the skin from the orange and roughly slice the flesh.

2 Push the orange, beetroot and carrot pieces alternately through a juicer, then add the spinach. Pour into glasses.

Cook's tip
Only use fresh, raw, firm beetroot for juicing, rather than the cooked variety – and most definitely avoid the pickled type in jars. Beetroot juice is a stunning, vibrant red and is surprisingly sweet, especially when mixed with carrot and orange juice.

Vitality juice

Fresh pears are a great energizer and can help give you a kick-start in the morning if you have a long, busy day ahead or a looming deadline to meet. This nutritious blend of ripe, juicy fruit, wheatgerm, yogurt, seeds and watercress makes a great-tasting tonic. If you would prefer a non-dairy version, use yogurt made from goat's milk, sheep's milk or soya.

Makes 1 large glass

25g/1oz watercress
1 large ripe pear
30ml/2 tbsp wheatgerm
150ml/¼ pint/⅔ cup natural (plain) yogurt
15ml/1 tbsp linseeds (flax seeds)
10ml/2 tsp lemon juice
mineral water (optional)
ice cubes

1 Roughly chop the watercress (you do not need to remove the tough stalks). Peel, core and roughly chop the pear.

2 Put the watercress and pear in a blender or food processor with the wheatgerm and blend until smooth. Scrape the mixture down from the side of the bowl if necessary.

Cook's tip
If you never have time for breakfast, prepare this juice in the evening and chill overnight. You can drink the juice on your journey into work and you'll then feel the benefits kick in throughout the day.

3 Add the yogurt, seeds and lemon juice and blend until evenly combined. Thin with a little mineral water if the mixture is too thick and pour over ice cubes. Decorate with watercress.

Iron crazy

This energizing drink contains spinach, apricots, carrots and pumpkin seeds, which are all rich in iron, as well as kelp, a type of seaweed, to give you an invigorating lift. Iron is essential for carrying oxygen in the blood and a shortage can quickly lead to tiredness and anaemia.

Makes 1 small glass

50g/2oz/¼ cup ready-to-eat dried apricots
15ml/1 tbsp pumpkin seeds
250g/9oz carrots
50g/2oz spinach
15ml/1 tbsp lemon juice
10ml/2 tsp kelp powder
mineral water
spinach leaf and pumpkin seeds, to decorate

Cook's tip
Sea vegetables are packed with minerals, protein and other valuable nutrients. Kelp is often sold in powder form, along with spirulina, a similarly nutrient-packed seaweed.

1 Chop the apricots finely, cover with 100ml/3½ fl oz/ scant ½ cup boiling water and leave for 10 minutes.

2 Using a large, sharp knife, carefully chop the pumpkin seeds into small pieces. (Take it slowly at first as the whole seeds have a tendency to scatter.) Roughly chop the carrots.

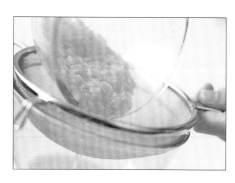

3 Drain the apricots. Push the spinach through a juicer, followed by the apricots and carrots. Stir in the lemon juice, pumpkin seeds and kelp powder.

4 Pour the juice into a glass, top up with a little mineral water, decorate with a spinach leaf and pumpkin seeds, then serve immediately for maximum benefit.

Body builder

Wheatgerm, the most nutritious part of the wheat grain, is packed with B and E vitamins, protein and minerals. Combined with bananas, it makes a great carbohydrate-rich drink that is boosted by the goodness of orange juice and linseeds and is perfect before exercise. Like all seeds, linseeds contain essential fatty acids that are good for the heart.

Makes 1 large glass

30ml/2 tbsp wheatgerm
1 large banana, chopped
130g/4½oz/generous ½ cup soya yogurt
15ml/1 tbsp linseeds (flax seeds)
juice of 1 lime
juice of 1 large orange
mineral water (optional)
linseeds and grated lime zest, to decorate

Cook's tip
Brewer's yeast is another healthy supplement that can be added to energy-boosting drinks. Rich in B vitamins and minerals, it is great for increasing vitality.

1 Put the wheatgerm, two-thirds of the banana, the yogurt and linseeds in a blender or food processor. Blend until smooth then, using a plastic spatula or spoon, scrape down the side of the bowl if necessary. Stir well.

2 Add the lime and orange juice to the yogurt mixture and blend again until evenly mixed. Pour the juice into a large glass and top up with mineral water. Decorate with linseeds, lime zest and the remaining banana, then serve.

Ginger juice

Fresh root ginger is one of the best natural cures for indigestion and it helps to settle upset stomachs, whether caused by food poisoning or motion sickness. In this unusual fruity blend, it is simply mixed with fresh, juicy pineapple and sweet-tasting carrot, creating a quick and easy remedy that can be juiced up in minutes – and tastes delicious too.

Makes 1 glass

½ small pineapple
25g/1oz fresh root ginger
1 carrot
ice cubes

Cook's tip
Before preparing the pineapple, turn it upside down and leave for half an hour – this makes it juicier.

1 Using a sharp knife, cut away the skin from the pineapple, then halve and remove the core. Roughly slice the pineapple flesh. Peel and roughly chop the ginger, then chop the carrot.

2 Push the carrot, ginger and pineapple through a juicer and pour into a glass. Add ice cubes and serve immediately.

Sleep easy

Some herbal teas are known for their purely soporific qualities, but this concoction is slightly more substantial – the last thing you want is to go to bed hungry. Blended bananas provide slow-release carbohydrates to sustain you through the night and lettuce is renowned for its sleep-inducing properties. It's just what you need when you want to relax.

1 Cover the teabag with 150ml/¼ pint/ ⅔ cup boiling water and leave to steep for 10 minutes. Meanwhile, chop the lettuce. Drain the teabag.

2 Chop the banana into a blender or food processor, add the lettuce and blend well until smooth, scraping the mixture down from the sides of the bowl, if necessary. Add the lemon juice and chamomile tea and blend briefly until smooth. Serve immediately.

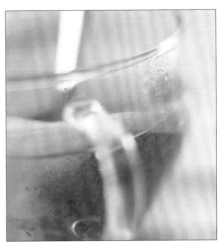

Makes 1 large glass

1 chamomile teabag
90g/3½oz iceberg lettuce
1 small banana
juice of ½ lemon

Cook's tip
If you have chamomile in the garden, use three or four flower-heads instead of the chamomile teabag. Let them steep in the boiling water for a few minutes, but don't leave them for too long or the flavour will become bitter.

vital
veggie
blends

When your energy levels are flagging, these drinks are guaranteed to perk you up. Made using pure vegetables with no additional additives, they serve a variety of purposes from detoxing and cleansing the body to healing and energizing the mind. Ready in minutes, blends including carrot, fennel, tomato and spinach are a sure-fire way to drink yourself healthy.

Bright eyes

Thin-skinned citrus fruits like clementines can be put through the juicer without peeling, adding a zesty kick to the final mix – and saving time when you're in a hurry. This vibrant, intensely flavoured carrot and clementine combination is packed with vitamin A, which is essential for healthy vision, and vitamin C to give an extra boost to the whole system.

1 Scrub the carrots and, using a sharp knife, chop them into large chunks of a similar size. Quarter the clementines, discarding any pips (seeds).

2 Push the clementine quarters through a juicer, then repeat the procedure with the carrot chunks.

3 Pour the juice over ice cubes in tall glasses and decorate each glass with a wedge or slice of clementine, if you like.

Makes 2 glasses

200g/7oz carrots
6 clementines, plus extra wedges or slices
  to decorate
ice cubes

Cook's tip
Take the tingle factor up a notch and add some extra zing by spicing up the mix a little. Peel and slice some fresh root ginger and push through the juicer with the clementines and carrots.

Smooth yet sassy, with all the colour of a brilliant golden sunrise, this mouthwatering juice will make waking up worthwhile – even on the most sluggish mornings.

Veggie boost

This simple blend makes a great juice boost. It has pure clean flavours and a chilli kick that is guaranteed to revitalize flagging energy levels. Tomatoes and carrots are rich in the valuable antioxidant betacarotene, which is reputed to fight cancer, and they contain a good supply of vitamins A, C and E, all of which are essential for good health.

Makes 2 glasses

3 tomatoes
1 fresh red or green chilli
250g/9oz carrots
juice of 1 orange
crushed ice

Cook's tip
Non-organic carrots often contain a lot of chemicals in their skins. If you use these, scrub them well or wash and peel them before use.

1 Quarter the tomatoes and roughly chop the chilli. (If you prefer a milder juice, remove the seeds and white pith from the chilli before chopping.) Scrub the carrots and chop them roughly.

2 Push the carrots through a juicer, then follow with the tomatoes and chilli. Add the orange juice and stir well to mix. Fill two tumblers with crushed ice, pour the juice over and serve.

Gazpacho juice

Inspired by the classic Spanish soup, this fabulous juice looks and tastes delicious. Fresh salad vegetables can be thrown into a blender or food processor and whizzed up in moments to create a refreshing, invigorating drink. If you are planning to invite friends for a relaxing al fresco lunch, serve this cooling juice as an appetizer; it is perfect for a hot summer's day.

Makes 4–5 glasses

½ fresh red chilli
800g/1¾lb tomatoes, skinned
½ cucumber, roughly sliced
1 red (bell) pepper, seeded and cut
   into chunks
1 celery stick, chopped
1 spring onion (scallion), roughly chopped
a small handful of fresh coriander (cilantro),
   stalks included, plus extra to decorate
juice of 1 lime
salt
ice cubes

1 Using a sharp knife, seed the chilli. Add to a blender or food processor with the tomatoes, cucumber, red pepper, celery, spring onion and coriander.

2 Blend well until smooth, scraping the vegetable mixture down from the side of the bowl, if necessary.

Cook's tip
Stir in a little extra tomato juice or mineral water if the juice is still thick after blending. A splash of red wine vinegar will intensify the flavour.

Juices made from fresh salad vegetables, packed full of valuable nutrients, are the ultimate thirst quenchers on a hot day, providing wonderfully fresh flavours and refreshing the palate instantly.

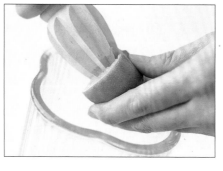

3 Add the lime juice and a little salt and blend. Pour into glasses. Add ice cubes and a few coriander leaves to serve.

Ruby roots

Beetroot has the highest sugar content of any vegetable and, not surprisingly, makes one of the most delicious, sweet juices, with a vibrant red colour and a rich yet refreshing taste. Despite its firm texture, beetroot can be juiced raw and its intense flavour combines wonderfully with tangy citrus fruits and fresh root ginger. Enjoy this juice as a natural cleanser.

Makes 1 large glass

200g/7oz raw beetroot (beets)
1cm/½in piece fresh root ginger, peeled
1 large orange
ice cubes

Cook's tip
Blood-red beetroot produces a vibrant, shockingly intense, jewel-coloured juice that is packed with vitamins and minerals, making it the perfect tonic and the ultimate health juice.

1 Trim the beetroot and cut into quarters. Push half through a juicer, followed by the ginger and remaining beetroot.

2 Squeeze the juice from the orange and mix with the beetroot juice.

3 Pour the juice over ice cubes in a glass or clear glass cup. Serve immediately.

Fennel fusion

This hefty combination of raw vegetables and apples makes a surprisingly delicious juice – fresh fennel has a distinctive aniseed flavour that blends well with both fruit and vegetables. Cabbage has natural anti-bacterial properties, while apples and fennel can help to cleanse the system. As an equally refreshing alternative, use two or three sticks of celery instead of the fennel.

Makes 1 glass

½ small red cabbage
½ fennel bulb
2 apples
15ml/1 tbsp lemon juice

Cook's tip
Buy really firm, fresh-looking fennel.
If left on the supermarket shelves, it
quickly discolours and turns fibrous.

1 Roughly slice the cabbage and fennel and quarter the apples. Using a juice extractor, juice the vegetables and fruit.

2 Add the lemon juice to the juice mixture and stir. Pour into a glass and serve immediately.

Apple and leaf lift-off

This delicious blend of apple, grapes, fresh leaves and lime juice is the perfect rejuvenator and is great for treating skin, liver and kidney disorders. Apples play a part in so many delicious and healthy blends that it's worth buying a large bag that will keep well in the refrigerator for several days. Most varieties can be juiced successfully so simply choose your favourite.

Makes 1 glass

1 apple
150g/5oz white grapes
small handful of fresh coriander (cilantro),
   stalks included
25g/1oz watercress or rocket (arugula)
15ml/1 tbsp lime juice

1 Using a sharp knife, quarter the apple, removing the core if you like. Using a juice extractor, juice the apples and grapes, followed by the coriander and the watercress or rocket.

2 Add the lime juice to the fruit and herb mixture and stir well. Pour the mixture into a tall glass and serve immediately for maximum flavour.

Mixed salad

Despite their reputation as being full of water, lettuce and cucumber contain important minerals such as calcium and zinc, alongside other crucial nutrients like vitamin K. Spinach contains plenty of betacarotene and has cancer-fighting properties. Juiced with ripe pears for maximum sweetness, a regular dose of this super juice can only enhance your health.

Makes 2–3 glasses

½ cucumber
½ iceberg, cos or romaine lettuce
2 large, ripe pears
75g/3oz fresh spinach
6–8 radishes
crushed ice
sliced radishes and cucumber, to decorate

Cook's tip
Although it can taste fairly bland in a salad, unpeeled cucumber has a surprisingly intense flavour when it is juiced. If you prefer a lighter taste, peel the cucumber with a sharp knife before juicing.

1 Using a small, sharp knife, chop the cucumber into chunks. Roughly tear the lettuce into pieces. Quarter the pears and remove the core.

2 Push all the ingredients through a juicer. Pour over crushed ice in tall glasses and serve with sliced radishes and cucumber swizzle sticks.

Orange blossom

Avocados are extremely good for the skin, mainly because of their high vitamin E content.
Combined with parsley, asparagus and orange, this juice makes a great cleanser and skin tonic.
If you have a particular skin problem, drinking this juice regularly should really make a difference
– it is extremely effective and much cheaper than many skin creams on the market.

2 Roughly chop the asparagus and add to the avocado. Blend thoroughly until smooth, scraping the mixture down from the side of the bowl, if necessary.

3 Juice the oranges and add to the mixture with the lemon juice. Blend briefly until the mixture is very smooth. Pour the juice into two glasses until two-thirds full, then add ice cubes and mineral water. Decorate with chunky orange wedges.

Cook's tip

The orange and lemon juice in this blend means that the avocados will not discolour, so you might want to refrigerate a glass for later on. If it has thickened slightly, stir in a little extra mineral water.

Makes 2 glasses

1 small avocado
small handful of parsley
75g/3oz tender asparagus spears
2 large oranges
squeeze of lemon juice
ice cubes
mineral water
orange wedges, to decorate

1 Halve the avocado and discard the stone (pit). Scoop the flesh into a blender or food processor. Remove any tough stalks from the parsley and add.

Sugar snap

Sweet and juicy sugar snap peas are one of the most delicious vegetables to serve raw and they taste just as good when put through a juicer. The sweetness of the peas and the melon intensifies when they are juiced and the fresh root ginger adds a certain edge to this mellow, cooling juice. Keep the melon in the refrigerator so that it's well and truly chilled when you come to blend the juice – you won't need to add ice.

Makes 1 large glass

1cm/½in piece fresh root ginger, peeled
¼ honeydew or Galia melon
200g/7oz sugar snap peas, including pods
melon chunks and peas, to decorate

Cook's tip
Use a fresh, plump-looking piece of ginger. If it is too old, it may have started to shrivel and won't produce the necessary juice and flavour.

1 Using a sharp knife, chop the ginger. Scoop out the seeds from the melon and cut it into wedges. Cut away the skin, then chop the flesh into chunks.

2 Push the sugar snap peas through a juicer, followed by the chunks of melon and the slices of ginger. Serve chilled, with melon chunks and peas.

Celery sensation

Savoury, almost salty, celery and sweet, green grapes make an astoundingly effective twosome when combined in a blended juice. A small handful of peppery watercress adds an extra punch, but be careful not to add too much because its flavour intensifies considerably when the leaves are juiced. Celery has one of the lowest calorie contents of all vegetables, so this is a particularly useful juice for anyone on a low-calorie diet.

Makes 1 large glass

2 celery sticks
a handful of watercress
200g/7oz/1¾ cups green grapes
1 leafy celery stick, to serve
crushed ice

1 Push the celery sticks through a juicer, followed by the watercress and the green grapes.

2 Put a leafy celery stick in a large glass to act as an edible swizzle stick and half-fill with crushed ice. Pour the juice over the ice and serve.

Broccoli booster

Hailed as a cure-all superfood and a vital ingredient in a healthy diet, broccoli's strong taste does, however, need a bit of toning down when juiced. Sweet and tangy apples and lemon juice soften its flavour, making a drink that's thoroughly enjoyable.

Makes 1 large glass

125g/4¼oz broccoli florets
2 eating apples
15ml/1 tbsp lemon juice
ice cubes

1 Cut the broccoli florets into small pieces and chop the apples.

2 Push both through a juicer and stir in the lemon juice. Serve in a tall glass with plenty of ice.

Cook's tip
Don't use the tough broccoli stalks as they provide little juice and don't have as good a flavour as the delicate florets. Broccoli is packed with antiviral and antibacterial nutrients and contains almost as much calcium as milk. It is also thought to prevent some cancers, so this juice is definitely worth drinking for its health benefits as well as its wonderful flavour.

Basil blush

Some herbs just don't juice well, losing their aromatic flavour and turning muddy and dull. Basil, however, is an excellent juicer, keeping its distinctive fresh fragrance. It makes the perfect partner for mild, refreshing cucumber and the ripest, juiciest tomatoes you can find.

Makes 1–2 glasses

½ cucumber, peeled
a handful of fresh basil, plus extra to decorate
350g/12oz tomatoes
ice cubes

Cook's tip
You don't have to peel the cucumber, but the juice will have a fresher, lighter colour without peel.

1 Quarter the cucumber lengthways – do not remove the seeds. Push it through a juicer with the basil, then do the same with the tomatoes.

2 Pour the blended tomato, basil and cucumber juice over cubes of ice in one or two glasses and serve decorated with a few fresh sprigs of basil.

fresh
and
fruity

Ripe, juicy fruits make fabulous drinks, whatever the
combination of ingredients but, if you're looking for
guidance, this stunning assortment of recipes will set
you off in a frenzy of fruity blending. Whether using
blackcurrants, bananas or exotic papayas, make
sure you use the pick of the crop so your juices are
both highly nutritious and tantalizingly tasty.

Pink and perky

This deliciously refreshing, rose-tinged blend of grapefruit and pear juice will keep you bright-eyed and bushy-tailed. It's perfect for a quick breakfast drink or as a pick-me-up later in the day when energy levels are flagging. If the grapefruit is particularly tart, serve with a little bowl of brown sugar to sweeten, or use brown sugar stirrers.

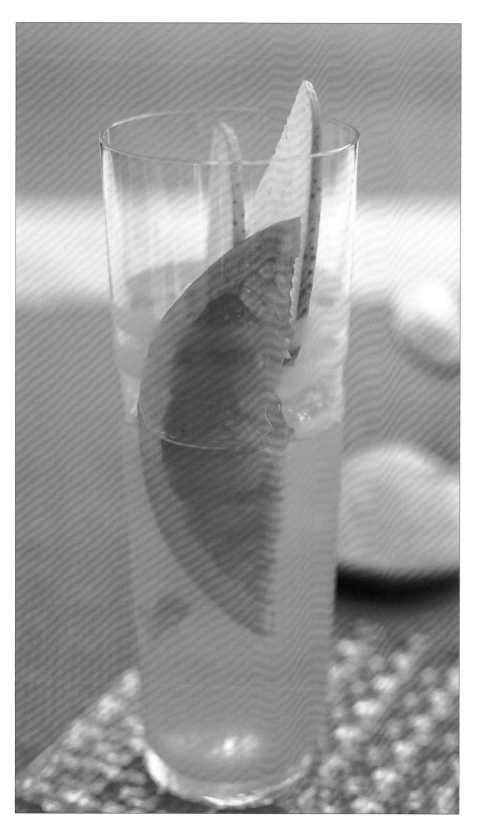

Makes 2 tall glasses

1 pink and 1 white grapefruit, halved
2 ripe pears
ice cubes

1 Take a thin slice from one grapefruit half and cut a few thin slices of pear. Roughly chop the remaining pear and push through a juicer.

2 Squeeze all the juice from the grapefruit halves. Mix the fruit juices together and serve over ice. Decorate with the grapefruit and pear slices.

Sweet, sharp shock

The taste-tingling combination of sweet red grape and tart apple is quite delicious. Grapes are full of natural sugars and, mixed with apple juice, they'll create a juice that's full of pep and zing. Grapes are also renowned for their cleansing properties, making this an ideal addition to any detox regime. For a longer, more refreshing drink, top up with sparkling mineral water.

1 Slice some grapes and a sliver or two of apple for the decoration. Roughly chop the remaining apples. Push through a juicer with the grapes.

2 Pour over crushed ice, decorate with the sliced fruit and serve immediately.

Makes 1 large glass

150g/5oz/1¼ cups red grapes
1 red-skinned eating apple
1 small cooking apple
crushed ice

Cook's tip
The simplest flavour combinations are often the most delicious. Sugary grapes together with mouth-puckeringly tart apples is one of those perfect pairings that simply cannot be beaten.

Hum-zinger

This tropical cleanser contains 100 per cent fruit. It will help boost the digestive system and the kidneys, making your eyes sparkle, your hair shine and your skin glow. For the best results, use really ripe fruit, otherwise the juice may be sharp and flavourless. If the fruit is not quite ripe when you buy it, leave it at room temperature for a day or two before juicing. If you like your juices really well chilled, serve with plenty of crushed ice.

Makes 1 glass

½ pineapple, peeled
1 small mango, peeled and pitted
½ small papaya, seeded and peeled

Cook's tip
Pineapple and mango can produce a very thick juice when blended so, if using this method, you might want to thin it down with a little mineral water before serving.

1 Remove any "eyes" left in the pineapple, then cut all the fruit into rough chunks. Using a juice extractor, juice all of the fruit.

2 Alternatively, use a food processor or blender and process for 2–3 minutes until very smooth. Pour into a glass and serve immediately.

Citrus sparkle

This vibrantly coloured juice is full of the goodness of natural citrus fruits. These zesty fruits are packed with immune-boosting vitamin C, which can help to ward off winter colds and put a spring in your step, along with valuable folic acid. They are also renowned for their digestive cleansing properties. If you find this blend a little too tart, try adding a delicious sweetener, such as honey, and mix the juice well before serving.

Makes 1 glass

1 pink grapefruit
1 orange
30ml/2 tbsp lemon juice

1 Using a sharp knife, cut the grapefruit and orange in half and squeeze out the juice using a citrus juicer.

2 Pour the mixed citrus juice into a tall glass, stir in the lemon juice and serve immediately.

Opposite: Hum-zinger (left) and Citrus sparkle (right)

Red defender

Boost your body's defences with this delicious blend of red fruits. Watermelon and strawberries are a good source of vitamin C and the black watermelon seeds, like all other seeds, are rich in essential nutrients. If you really don't like the idea of blending the seeds, remove them first.

1 Hull the strawberries and halve them if they are large. Pull the grapes from their stalks. Cut away the skin from the watermelon.

2 Put the watermelon in a blender or food processor and blend until the seeds are broken up. Add the strawberries and grapes and blend until completely smooth, scraping the mixture down from the side of the bowl, if necessary. Serve in tall glasses.

Makes 2 glasses

200g/7oz/1¾ cups strawberries
small bunch red grapes, about 90g/3½oz
1 small wedge of watermelon

Cook's tip
Decorate this juice with chunks of watermelon or strawberry halves.

Apricot squash

The availability of fresh apricots can be rather erratic, so buy lots when you see them and make delicious apricot-based juices like this one. Choose sweet and juicy, ripe apricots, as they will act as a perfect foil to the tangy limes in this refreshing drink.

Makes 2 glasses

2 limes
3 oranges
4 ripe apricots
several sprigs of lemon balm, plus extra
    to decorate

Cook's tip
This makes a tangy, invigorating blend to wake up your senses. Stir in a little honey or sugar if you find it a bit too tart.

1 Squeeze the limes and oranges, either by hand or using a citrus juicer. Halve and stone (pit) the apricots.

2 Put the apricots in a blender or food processor with a little of the citrus juice and the lemon balm, and blend until smooth, scraping the mixture down from the side of the bowl, if necessary. Add the remaining juice and blend until completely smooth.

3 Pour into medium glasses and serve decorated with extra lemon balm.

Apple shiner

Enjoy radiant skin and an instant energy boost with this cleansing fusion of apple, honeydew melon, red grapes and lemon. This is a good drink to make in the spring, when all of these fruits are widely available. If you cannot get hold of honeydew melon, however, you can use any other type as a substitute in this juice, as long as it's ripe.

Makes 1 glass

½ honeydew melon
1 apple
90g/3½ oz red grapes
15ml/1 tbsp lemon juice

Cook's tip
This drink is refreshingly sharp and tangy, but if you use really sweet apple and melon you might want to add a dash more lemon juice. Taste and see before serving.

1 Using a sharp knife, cut the melon into quarters, scoop out the seeds with a spoon and slice the flesh away from the skin. Quarter the apple and remove the core if you like.

2 Using a juicer, juice the fruit. Alternatively, process the fruit in a food processor or blender for 2–3 minutes until smooth. Pour the juice into a glass, stir in the lemon juice and serve.

Melon pick-me-up

This spicy blend of melon, pear and fresh root ginger will revive your body, stimulate your circulation and fire you into action. It is a great drink to serve at any time of day, whether you're relaxing with a late breakfast or reviving flagging energy levels at the end of a day's work. Serve really chilled, adding some crushed ice or ice cubes if you like.

Makes 1 glass

2 pears
½ cantaloupe melon
2.5cm/1in piece of fresh root ginger

1 Using a sharp knife, quarter the pears. Slice the melon in half and scoop out the seeds with a spoon. Cut the flesh away from the skin, then quarter.

2 Using a juicer, juice all the ingredients, pour into a tall glass and serve immediately.

Opposite: Apple shiner (left) and Melon pick-me-up (right)

Blue lagoon

Blueberries are not only an excellent source of betacarotene and vitamin C, they are also rich in flavonoids, which help to cleanse the system. Mixed with other dark red fruits, such as blackberries and grapes, they make a highly nutritious and extremely delicious blend that can be stored in the refrigerator and relished throughout the day.

1 Pull the blackcurrants, if using, and grapes from their stalks.

2 Push the fruits through a juicer, saving a few for decoration. Place the ice in a medium glass and pour over the juice. Decorate with the remaining fruit and serve.

Makes 1 glass

90g/3½oz/scant 1 cup blackcurrants
  or blackberries
150g/5oz red grapes
130g/4½oz/generous 1 cup blueberries
ice cubes

Cook's tip
This is a really tangy wake-up drink that you might find a bit too sharp. Add a dash of sugar or honey, or top up with mineral water to dilute it slightly, if you like.

Pomegranate plus

Sometimes difficult to find, pomegranates are worth buying when you see them because their exotic and distinctive flavour is quite delicious. A reddish skin is usually a sign that the seeds inside will be vibrant and sweet. Pomegranate juice makes a delicious base for this treat of a juice, which is mildly spiced with a hint of fresh ginger.

Makes 2 glasses

2 pomegranates
4 fresh figs
15g/½oz fresh root ginger, peeled
10ml/2 tsp lime juice
ice cubes and lime wedges, to serve

Cook's tip
Pomegranates are refreshing in hot weather, especially when juiced with figs, ginger and lime juice. Serve ice-cold to quench a summer thirst.

1 Halve the pomegranates. Working over a bowl to catch the juices, pull away the skin to remove the jewel-like clusters of seeds.

2 Quarter the figs and roughly chop the ginger. Push the figs and ginger through a juicer. Push the pomegranate seeds through, reserving a few for decoration. Stir in the lime juice. Pour over ice cubes and lime wedges, then serve.

Tropical calm

This deliciously scented juice is packed with the cancer-fighting antioxidant betacarotene and can aid liver and kidney function to cleanse and purify the system. This is a quick and easy drink to make at any time of day, whether you're rushing out in the morning or relaxing later in the day. If you're really thirsty, it's a good blend to top up with plenty of chilled sparkling water.

Makes 1 glass

1 papaya
½ cantaloupe melon
90g/3½ oz white grapes

Cook's tip
Some varieties of papaya stay green when ripe, but most turn yellowy-orange and soften slightly. They bruise easily so don't buy any that have been knocked about. The seeds are edible but not particularly tasty, so they are usually discarded.

1 Using a sharp knife, halve and skin the papaya, remove the seeds and then cut the flesh into rough slices. Halve the melon, scoop out the seeds and cut into quarters. Slice the flesh away from the skin and cut into chunks.

2 Juice the fruit using a juicer, or blend in a food processor or blender for a thicker juice. Serve immediately.

Strawberry soother

Juices don't come much purer than this one. Made with fresh, ripe strawberries and a delicious peach or nectarine, depending on your preference, nothing else at all is added to this comforting blend. Rich in vitamin C, calcium and healing phytochemicals, strawberries are a good addition to any detox diet, while peaches and nectarines are great for healthy skin.

Makes 1 glass

1 peach or nectarine
225g/8oz/2 cups strawberries

1 Using a sharp knife, quarter the peach or nectarine and pull out the stone (pit). Cut the flesh into rough slices or chunks ready for juicing. Hull the strawberries.

2 Juice the fruit, using a juicer, or blend in a food processor or blender for a thicker juice. Serve immediately.

Opposite: Tropical calm (left) and Strawberry soother (right)

Minty melon cooler

The wonderfully juicy flesh of ripe melon seems somehow more fragrant and sweet when juiced. A dash of lime cuts through the sweetness perfectly and zips up the flavour, while refreshing, peppery mint makes a classic, cool companion to both. This mellow soother is equally calming and stimulating – what a combination.

Makes 3–4 glasses

1 Galia or cantaloupe melon
several large mint sprigs
juice of 2 large limes
ice cubes
extra mint sprigs and lime slices, to decorate

1 Halve and seed the melon and cut into wedges. Cut one wedge into long, thin slices and reserve for decoration.

2 Cut the skin from the remaining melon wedges and push half the melon through a juicer. Strip the mint leaves from the sprigs, push them through the juicer, then juice the remaining melon.

3 Stir in the lime juice and then pour the juice over ice cubes in glasses. Decorate with mint sprigs and lime slices. Add a slice of melon to each glass and serve.

Cherry berry trio

Strawberries and grapes have long been reputed to cleanse and purify the system, while cherries and strawberries are rich in vitamin C. This trio of plump, ripe fruits is packed with natural fruit sugars and needs absolutely no sweetening. To really spoil yourself (and undo all that cleansing power), try adding a splash of your favourite orange liqueur.

Makes 2 large glasses

200g/7oz/1¾ cups strawberries
250g/9oz/2¼ cups red grapes
150g/5oz/1¼ cups red cherries, pitted
ice cubes

Cook's tip
Each year, the cherry season passes all too swiftly, so enjoy them in their full glory in this refreshing blend of sweet, fruity, fragrant red juices.

1 Halve two or three strawberries and grapes and set aside with a few perfect cherries for decoration. Cut up any large strawberries, then push through a juicer with the remaining grapes and cherries.

2 Pour into glasses, top with the halved fruits, cherries and ice cubes, and serve immediately. To make a fun decoration, skewer a halved strawberry or grape on a cocktail stick (toothpick) and hang a cherry by its stem.

No gooseberry fool

Combine a sharp, tangy fruit like gooseberries with the sweetness of apples, greengages and kiwi fruit for a perfect blend of flavours – not too sweet, not too sharp, in fact just perfect. Even better, this drink is 100 per cent natural and is loaded with vital vitamins and minerals, meaning you can enjoy this delicious healthy tonic at any time of the day – guilt-free.

1 Peel the kiwi fruit, then halve and stone (pit) the greengages. Core and roughly chop the apple.

2 Push the kiwi fruit, greengages, apple and gooseberries through a juicer and pour over ice cubes into a glass. Add one or two gooseberries to decorate.

Makes 1 glass

1 kiwi fruit
2 greengages
1 eating apple
90g/3½oz/scant 1 cup gooseberries, plus
   extra to decorate
ice cubes

Cook's tip
Pink-tinged dessert gooseberries tend to be sweeter than the green ones, but both taste good in this refreshing drink. You might want to freeze a punnet of gooseberries so that you have a handy supply.

Golden wonder

Ripe plums make delicious juices and work really well with the banana and passion fruit in this unconventional blend. Use yellow plums if you can find them, as they are irresistibly sweet and juicy, but red ones can easily be substituted as long as they're really soft and ripe. Vitamin-rich and energizing, this drink is sure to set you up for the day.

Makes 1 large glass

2 passion fruit
2 yellow plums
1 small banana
about 15ml/1 tbsp lemon juice

Cook's tip
Passion fruit seeds might look pretty in a fruit juice, but they are not to everyone's taste. If you prefer a juice without seeds, press the pulp through a small sieve before adding to the blender.

1 Halve the passion fruit and, using a teaspoon, scoop the pulp into a blender or food processor. Using a small, sharp knife, halve and stone (pit) the plums and add to the blender or food processor.

2 Add the banana and lemon juice and blend the mixture until smooth, scraping the mixture down from the side of the bowl, if necessary. Pour into a large glass and check the sweetness. Add a little more lemon juice, if you like.

extra
exotic
coolers

Take juicing and blending into another league altogether with these enticing, adventurous and utterly irresistible creations. Try delicious sun-dried tomatoes with orange and tarragon or fabulous ripe pomegranates with Asian pears. Start experimenting and you'll soon discover that the possibilities are endless.

Apple infusion

East meets West in this fabulous fusion of fresh apple and fragrant spices. Ginger is combined with apple juice and exotic, fragrant lemon grass to make a deliciously refreshing cooler.
As with many of these juices, it is well worth making double the quantity and keeping a supply in the refrigerator – as you will undoubtedly be back for more.

2 Roughly chop the root ginger and cut the apples into chunks. Push the ginger and then the apples through a juicer.

3 Pour the juice into the jug and place in the refrigerator for at least 1 hour to let the flavours infuse.

4 Half-fill two or three tall glasses with ice cubes and red apple slices, if you like, and pour in the juice until it just covers the ice. Top up with sparkling water or lemonade, if you prefer, and serve immediately.

Makes 2–3 glasses

1 lemon grass stalk
15g/½oz fresh root ginger, peeled
4 red-skinned eating apples
ice cubes
sparkling water or real lemonade
red apple slices, to decorate

Cook's tip
Bruising the lemon grass stalk releases the subtle flavour, which pervades this cooler and provides a fragrant hint of the East.

1 Bruise the lemon grass stalk by pounding it with the tip of a rolling pin. Make several lengthways cuts through the stalk to open it up, keeping it intact at the thick end. Put the bruised stem into a small glass jug (pitcher).

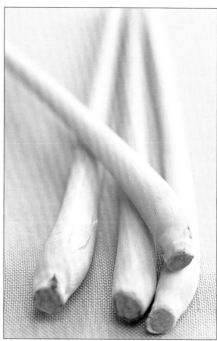

Lavender orange lush

This fragrant, lavender-scented juice is guaranteed to perk up a jaded palate in no time at all. Its heavenly aroma and distinct yet subtle taste is quite divine. Make plenty and keep it in the refrigerator, adding a few extra lavender sprigs to intensify the flavour, if you like. Additional sprigs of lavender make fun stirrers or a pretty garnish if serving at a party.

Makes 4–6 glasses

10–12 lavender flowers, plus extra to serve
45ml/3 tbsp caster (superfine) sugar
8 large oranges
ice cubes

Cook's tip
This is an ideal drink to prepare for friends on a summer evening. Just pour into ice-cold glasses and then sit back and relax.

1 Pull the lavender flowers from their stalks and put them in a bowl with the sugar plus 120ml/4fl oz/½ cup boiling water. Stir until the sugar has dissolved, then leave to steep for 10 minutes.

2 Squeeze the oranges using a citrus juicer and pour the juice into a jug (pitcher). Strain the lavender syrup into the juice and chill.

3 Put a few ice cubes and a couple of lavender stirrers in some glasses, top up with the juice and serve.

Fragrant fruits

This blend of sweet and subtle fruits packs a surprising punch. It combines a splash of lemon and a hint of fresh root ginger to add zest and bite without overpowering the delicate, fragrant flavours of lychee, cantaloupe and pear. Other types of melon can be used in place of the cantaloupe, but you will lose the pretty colour that is part of this juice's appeal.

Makes 2 tall glasses

10 lychees
1 large pear
300g/11oz wedge cantaloupe melon,
   rind removed
2cm/¾in piece fresh root ginger,
   roughly chopped
squeeze of lemon juice
crushed ice
mint sprigs, to decorate

1 Peel and stone (pit) the lychees and, using a sharp knife, cut both the pear and the melon into large chunks.

2 Push the ginger through a juicer, followed by the lychees, pear and melon. Sharpen the flavour with a little of the lemon juice to taste.

3 Place the crushed ice and one or two mint sprigs in tall glasses and pour over the juice. Place some more mints sprigs on top to decorate, then serve the juice immediately – before the ice melts.

Cook's tip
Sweet, scented lychee and perfectly ripe cantaloupe melon shine through in this gloriously fragrant, delicately coloured blend of fresh fruits. To say that this drink is simply delicious is understating its qualities – not only is it subtle and refreshing, it is also extremely good for you. If you want to be a little wicked, however, add a dash of vodka – it will add an extra special kick.

Pink gin

Juniper berries are a vital ingredient in the making of gin and, not surprisingly, they exude distinct gin-like aromas in this fabulous drink. For a good colour, this is best made using early, forced rhubarb, which gives the juice a characteristic pink blush. Top up the gin with chilled sparkling water, or use real lemonade for a delicious, tangy taste.

Makes 4 glasses

600g/1lb 6oz rhubarb
finely grated rind and juice of 2 limes
75g/3oz/6 tbsp caster (superfine) sugar
15ml/1 tbsp juniper berries, lightly crushed
ice cubes
lime slices, quartered
sparkling mineral water, soda water (club soda) or real lemonade

1 Using a sharp knife, chop the rhubarb into 2cm/¾in lengths and place in a pan with the lime rind and juice.

2 Add the sugar, crushed juniper berries and 90ml/6 tbsp water. Cover with a tightly fitting lid and cook for 6–8 minutes until the rhubarb is just tender. (Test by prodding the rhubarb with the tip of a knife.)

3 Transfer the rhubarb to a food processor or blender and process to form a smooth purée. Press the mixture through a coarse sieve into a bowl and set the strained juice aside until completely cooled.

4 Half-fill medium glasses with the juice. Add ice cubes and lime slices and top up with sparkling mineral water, soda water or lemonade. Serve immediately.

Cook's tip

If the rhubarb syrup is stored for a couple of days in the refrigerator after straining, the juniper flavour will become more pronounced. The overall intensity is better if the drink is made with just rhubarb, but you could use a mixture of apple and rhubarb, if you prefer.

Passion fruit and orange crush

The scent and taste of this juice achieves that perfect balance of aromas and flavours. Sweet, zesty orange juice sits in perfect harmony with aromatic cardamom and intensely fragrant passion fruit to make the most heavenly juice imaginable. And, as well as the fabulous flavour and glorious colour, you get a generous shot of valuable vitamin C.

Makes 2 glasses

15ml/1 tbsp cardamom pods
15ml/1 tbsp caster (superfine) sugar
2 passion fruit
4 large oranges
ice cubes
halved orange slices, to decorate

1 Crush the cardamom pods in a mortar with a pestle or place them in a small, metal bowl and pound with the end of a rolling pin until the seeds are exposed.

2 Tip the cardamom pods, with any stray seeds, into a small pan. Add the sugar and stir in 90ml/6 tbsp water. Cover and simmer for 5 minutes.

Cook's tip
The dark seeds in passion fruit look pretty when suspended in the juice and are perfectly edible, but they do not offer any nutrition and can get stuck between your teeth. If you don't want them in the drink, press the pulp through a small sieve with the back of a wooden spoon and just use the juice.

Sweet yet sharp, delicate yet robust, mouth-puckering yet refreshing – each and every sip of this unbelievably delicious blend will delight you.

3 Halve the passion fruit and scoop the pulp into a small jug (pitcher). Squeeze the oranges in a citrus juicer or by hand and tip the juice into the jug. Strain the cardamom syrup through a fine sieve into the fruit juice and whisk the mixture to distribute the passion fruit and make a light froth.

4 Half-fill tall glasses with ice cubes and pour over the juice. Slip the orange slices into the glasses to serve as edible decoration.

Honey and watermelon tonic

This refreshing juice will help to cool the body, calm the digestion and cleanse the system – and may even have aphrodisiac qualities. What more could you ask from a juice? It even looks enticing. The real magic of this drink, however, lies in its flavour. The light, watermelon taste is fresh on the palate, while the sticky, warm honey warms the throat – but it is the tart lime that gives it that edge.

Makes 4 glasses

1 watermelon
1 litre/1¾ pints/4 cups chilled water
juice of 2 limes
clear honey
ice cubes, to serve

1 Using a sharp knife, chop the watermelon into chunks, cutting off the skin and discarding the black seeds.

2 Place the watermelon chunks in a large bowl, pour the chilled water over and leave to stand for 10 minutes.

3 Strain the watermelon chunks, then push them through a juicer.

4 Stir in the lime juice and sweeten to taste with honey. Pour into a jug (pitcher), add ice cubes and stir. Serve in wide, chunky glasses.

Cook's tip

If the weather is really hot, why not serve this as a frozen slush? Freeze, stirring often, and when crystals begin to form serve immediately.

Watermelon and star anise fizz

The delicate taste of watermelon becomes surprisingly intense when juiced, so to balance it, additional flavours need to be equally pronounced. A light syrup infused with scented star anise is the perfect choice. For maximum impact, make sure the star anise is really fresh as its liquorice-like flavour and aroma tend to fade with age.

1 Roughly crush the star anise in a mortar using a pestle, or place it in a small metal bowl and pound with the end of a rolling pin.

2 Tip the crushed spice into a small pan and add the sugar and 90ml/ 6 tbsp water. Bring to the boil, stirring, then let it bubble for about 2 minutes. Remove the pan from the heat and leave to steep for 10 minutes.

3 Cut off and discard the rind from the watermelon and, using a small, sharp knife, cut the flesh into chunks of roughly the same size, removing all of the hard black seeds.

4 Push the melon chunks through a juicer. Strain the anise syrup through a fine sieve and pour it into the melon juice. Stir well to mix the flavours together thoroughly.

5 Fill two glasses two-thirds full with the juice, then top up with sparkling water and serve immediately.

Makes 2 tall glasses

15g/½oz star anise
15ml/1 tbsp caster (superfine) sugar
500g/1¼lb wedge of watermelon
sparkling mineral water

Cook's tip
Sweet, scented, frothy pink bubbles make this heavenly juice perfect as a non-alcoholic cocktail to serve at parties. Or enjoy it as a cooling thirst-quencher on a long, hot summer afternoon.

Kiwi and stem ginger spritzer

The delicate, refreshingly tangy flavour of kiwi fruit becomes sweeter and more intense when the flesh is juiced. Choose plump, unwrinkled fruits that give a little when gently pressed as under-ripe fruits will produce a slightly bitter taste. A single kiwi fruit contains more than one day's vitamin C requirement, so this juice will really boost the system.

Makes 1 tall glass

2 kiwi fruit
1 piece preserved stem ginger, plus 15ml/
   1 tbsp syrup from the ginger jar
sparkling mineral water

2 Push the ginger and kiwi fruit through a juicer and pour the juice into a jug (pitcher). Stir in the ginger syrup.

3 Pour the juice into a tall glass, then top up with sparkling mineral water and serve immediately.

Cook's tip

Kiwis are a subtropical fruit, not a tropical one, so it is best to store them in the refrigerator before using. If you want them to ripen quickly, store in a closed plastic bag with an apple, pear or banana.

1 Using a sharp knife, roughly chop the kiwi fruit and the ginger. (For a better colour you can peel the kiwi fruit first, but this is not essential.)

Spiced pomegranate and Asian pear fizz

Sweet but with a milder flavour than traditional pears, Asian pears make a good partner for the fresh tang of pomegranates. Juice the fruits in advance if you have the time, so the spice can mellow into the fruits, all ready for topping up with fizzy tonic water.

Makes 2 glasses

2 Asian pears
1.5ml/¼ tsp ground allspice
1 pomegranate
5–10ml/1–2 tsp clear honey
ice cubes
tonic water
pear wedges and pomegranate seeds,
   to decorate

Cook's tip

Ideal for slimmers, pears are virtually fat-free and contain absolutely no cholesterol or sodium. They also provide significant amounts of vitamin C and potassium.

1 Using a small, sharp knife, chop the pears into large chunks. Mix the allspice in a jug (pitcher) with 15ml/ 1 tbsp boiling water.

2 Halve the pomegranate. Working over the jug to catch the juices, peel away the skin and layers of pith to leave the clusters of seeds.

3 Push the pears and pomegranate seeds through a juicer and mix together in the jug with the allspice. Stir in a little honey to sweeten, then chill.

4 Pour the juice into glasses until two-thirds full. Serve with ice cubes, pear wedges and pomegranate seeds to decorate. Top up with tonic water.

Elderflower, plum and ginger juice

Captured in cordials and juices, the aromatic flavour of elderflowers can be enjoyed all year round. Here it is used with fresh root ginger to give an exotic boost to sweet, juicy plums. Serve this juice just as it is over plenty of crushed ice or top up with sparkling water, if you prefer a more diluted drink. It is an utterly delicious and wonderfully uplifting blend.

Makes 2–3 glasses

15g/½oz fresh root ginger
500g/1lb 2oz ripe plums
125ml/4½fl oz/generous ½ cup sweetened
   elderflower cordial
ice cubes
sparkling water or tonic water
mint sprigs and plum slices, to decorate

Cook's tip

The elder is a tree or bush with perfumed, yellowish-white flowers and tiny black-violet berries, both of which are thought to be medicinal.

1 Roughly chop the ginger without peeling. Halve and stone (pit) the plums.

2 Push half the plums through a juicer, followed by the ginger then the remaining plums. Mix the juice with the elderflower cordial in a jug (pitcher).

3 Place the ice cubes into two large or three medium-sized glasses. Pour over the juice until the glasses are two-thirds full. Place the mint sprigs and plum slices on top to decorate and top up with sparkling mineral water or tonic water. Serve immediately.

Thyme-scented plum lush

Make this divine drink in the early autumn when plums are at their sweetest and best. Their silky smooth flesh blends down to produce the most wonderfully textured smoothie, while delicately scented lemon thyme and honey complement the flavour perfectly. This luxurious juice is easy to make and has an irresistible fragrance that is at once warming and refreshing.

Makes 2–3 glasses

400g/14oz red plums
30–45ml/2–3 tbsp clear honey
15ml/1 tbsp chopped fresh lemon thyme,
    plus extra thyme sprigs to decorate
100g/3¾oz crushed ice

Cook's tip
Dark, purplish-red plums, with their almost violet bloom and sweet, intense flavour, juice well and make some of the most tempting and vibrant fruit drinks.

1 Using a sharp knife, halve and stone (pit) the plums and put in a blender or food processor. Add 30ml/2 tbsp of the honey and the lemon thyme and blend until smooth, scraping down the side of the bowl, if necessary.

2 Add the ice and blend until slushy. Taste for sweetness, adding a little more honey if necessary. Pour into glasses and serve immediately, decorated with a sprig of thyme.

Iced pear aniseed

Aniseed is a spice widely used in cooking, not only in sweet and savoury dishes but as the dominant flavour in many alcoholic drinks like pastis, ouzo and raki. If these flavours appeal to you – without the alcohol, though – you'll love this deliciously spicy pear-based infusion. Serve in small glasses over plenty of crushed ice. Add a slice or two of fresh pear, if you like.

Makes 2–3 glasses

30ml/2 tbsp aniseeds
30ml/2 tbsp caster (superfine) sugar
3 soft, ripe pears
10ml/2 tsp lemon juice
crushed ice

1 Using a mortar and pestle, lightly crush the aniseeds. (Alternatively, use a small bowl and the end of a rolling pin to crush the seeds.) Put in a small pan with the sugar and 100ml/3½fl oz/ scant ½ cup water. Heat very gently, stirring until the sugar has dissolved. Bring to the boil and boil for 1 minute. Pour the syrup into a small jug (pitcher) and leave to cool completely.

2 Quarter the pears and remove the cores. Push through a juicer. Add the lemon juice. Strain the syrup into the pear juice and chill until ready to serve. Pour over crushed ice in small glasses.

Cook's tip
For a great-tasting juice that really packs a punch, make sure you use fresh, sweet pears as underripe ones will result in a disappointing and almost bland juice.

It is also important to use fresh and aromatic aniseed. Like all herbs and spices, aniseed loses its flavour extremely quickly and, when it turns stale, it lacks flavour and has a slightly musty aroma, which could ruin your drink.

Red hot chilli pepper

Sweet red peppers make a colourful, light juice that's best mixed with other ingredients for a full flavour impact. Courgettes add a subtle, almost unnoticeable body to the drink, while chilli and radishes add a wonderful kick of peppery heat. Freshly squeezed orange juice gives a delicious underlying zest to this extremely drinkable beverage.

1 Halve the red peppers, remove the cores and seeds, quarter the pieces and push them through a juicer with the chilli. Cut the courgettes into chunks, halve the radishes and push them through the juicer.

2 Squeeze the orange and stir the juice into the vegetable juice. Fill two or three glasses with ice, pour over the juice and serve immediately.

Makes 2–3 glasses

2 red (bell) peppers
1 fresh red chilli, seeded
150g/5oz courgettes (zucchini)
75g/3oz radishes
1 orange
ice cubes

Cook's tip
When working with chillies, always wash your hands thoroughly after chopping them. Avoid touching your eyes or any other delicate area because it really will sting.

Tarragon, orange and sun-dried tomato juice

Lovers of tomato juice are sure to get hooked on this flavour-packed, vitalizing blend. Fresh orange makes it irresistibly moreish and adds extra vitamin C, while tarragon adds a lovely aromatic note. Add a dash of Tabasco or chilli sauce instead of the ground black pepper if you simply cannot resist the classic combination of chilli and tomato.

Makes 2 glasses

4 large sprigs of tarragon, plus extra to garnish
500g/1lb 2oz tomatoes
2 large oranges
15ml/1 tbsp sun-dried tomato paste
ice cubes
ground black pepper

1 Pull the tarragon leaves from their stalks. Roughly chop the tomatoes. Push them through a juicer, alternating with the tarragon leaves.

2 Squeeze the juice from the oranges by hand or using a citrus juicer. Stir into the tomato and tarragon juice. Add the sun-dried tomato paste and stir well to mix all the ingredients together.

3 Place ice cubes into two glasses and pour over the juice. Serve immediately with pretty stirrers (if you have them), a sprinkling of black pepper to taste and tarragon sprigs to garnish.

easy
breakfast
blends

Breakfast is the most important meal of the day but also the most neglected, so give yourself a kick-start with these fuel-packed, imaginative drinks. Made in minutes and easier to digest than a bowl of cereal, fabulous fresh fruit juices and decadent mocha smoothies provide the perfect early-morning boost.

Citrus tingler

With a reliable abundance of oranges available throughout the year, it is all too easy to overlook the more unusual citrus fruits. This citrus trio combines the sharp, grapefruit-like fragrance of pomelos, the mild sweetness of Ugli fruit and the vibrant colour of flavour-packed mandarins.

1 Halve the fruits and squeeze the juice using a citrus juicer. Add a little squeeze of lemon or lime juice, if you like, to create a sharper flavour.

2 Pour the juice into a tall glass and add ice cubes and a few citrus fruit slices to decorate. Serve immediately.

Makes 1 glass

1 pomelo
1 Ugli fruit
1 mandarin
squeeze of lemon or lime juice (optional)
ice cubes
citrus fruit slices, to decorate

Cook's tip
If you are making breakfast for your partner or the family, simply multiply the ingredients by the number of people that you are serving – or even better, let them make their own.

Morning after

A Bloody Mary is a traditional hangover cure with a reputation for actually working. Spicy, refreshing and mildly alcoholic – if you can face it – this version will invigorate sluggish energy levels with a generous dose of vitamin C and antioxidants to cleanse your system.

Makes 1 glass

300g/11oz ripe tomatoes
5ml/1 tsp Tabasco or Worcestershire sauce
5ml/1 tsp lemon juice
15–30ml/1–2 tbsp vodka (optional)
crushed ice
celery leaves, to decorate

Cook's tip
You don't need to have a hangover to enjoy this rich, refreshing drink, but if you want to have it for breakfast on a regular basis, it's best to leave out the vodka.

1 Roughly chop the tomatoes and push through a juicer.

2 Add the Tabasco or Worcestershire sauce, lemon juice and vodka, if using. Pour over plenty of crushed ice in a large glass. Add a few celery leaves and serve immediately.

Creamy banana boost

Bananas are a great energy food. They are packed with valuable nutrients and healthy carbohydrates, and they also fill you up – which is definitely a bonus. Blended with the additional fruits – pineapple, dates and lemon juice – and creamy milk, this delicious concoction will keep you going for hours. If you're prone to snacking throughout the day, try this and you'll feel all the better for it. Any leftover drink can be stored in the refrigerator for up to a day.

Makes 2–3 tall glasses

½ pineapple
4 Medjool dates, pitted
1 small ripe banana
juice of 1 lemon
300ml/½ pint/1¼ cups very cold full cream
   (whole) milk or soya milk

Cook's tip
The Medjool date is considered to be the jewel of all dates because of its size, texture and sweetness. It originates from Morocco, where it was reserved for royal hosts and other dignitaries centuries ago. Nowadays we can all enjoy them.

1 Using a small, sharp knife, cut away the skin and core from the pineapple. Roughly chop the flesh and put it in a blender or food processor, then add the pitted dates.

2 Peel and chop the banana and add it to the rest of the fruit together with the lemon juice.

3 Blend thoroughly until smooth, stopping to scrape the mixture down from the side of the bowl with a rubber spatula, if necessary.

4 Add the milk to the blender or food processor and process briefly until well combined. Pour the smoothie into tall glasses and serve immediately.

Zesty soya smoothie

Whizzed up with freshly squeezed orange juice, a splash of tangy lemon and a little fragrant honey, tofu can be transformed into a drink that's smooth, creamy, nutritious and delicious. Most people would not think to add tofu to a blended drink, but please do try it – you will be genuinely surprised. If possible, try to get hold of some silken tofu for this smoothie, as it has a wonderful satiny texture that blends particularly well.

Makes 1 large glass

2 oranges
15ml/1 tbsp lemon juice
20–25ml/4–5 tsp sunflower honey or
   herb honey
150g/5oz tofu
long, thin strips of pared orange rind,
   to decorate

Cook's tip
If you prefer a smooth drink, strain the liquid through a sieve after blending to remove the orange rind.

1 Finely grate the rind of one orange and set aside. Use a citrus juicer to juice both oranges and pour the juice into a food processor or blender. Add the grated orange rind, lemon juice, sunflower or herb honey and tofu.

2 Whizz the ingredients until smooth and creamy, then pour into a glass. Decorate with the pared orange rind and serve.

Opposite: Creamy banana boost (left) and Zesty soya smoothie (right)

Dairy-free deluxe

Prunes, apples, oranges and soya milk may seem like an unusual combination but the results are absolutely fabulous. Sweet, caramel-rich and very drinkable, this is a great milkshake for both adults and children, and, of course, for anyone on a dairy-free diet. Regular cow's milk can be used, if you prefer, but if you are watching the calories, use skimmed milk. The resulting drink will not be quite as creamy, but it will still be delicious.

Makes 1 tall glass

2 small eating apples
5 ready-to-eat pitted prunes
juice of 1 orange
60ml/4 tbsp soya milk
ice cubes

Cook's tip
Any eating apples can be used for this drink. If you prefer a tart flavour opt for a Granny Smith or a Cox's Pippin; if not, go for a sweet apple like the Royal Gala.

1 Using a small, sharp knife, remove the core from the apples and chop into chunks – but do not peel them. Push half the chopped apple through a juicer, followed by the prunes and the remaining chopped apple.

2 Pour the apple and prune juice into a jug (pitcher) and add the orange juice and soya milk. Whisk lightly until smooth and frothy. Pour into a chunky glass and serve immediately, adding a few cubes of ice.

Pear flair

For a truly refreshing combination, you can't do much better than a mixture of juicy pears and grapes. Wheatgerm adds body for a sustained energy fix and soya yogurt turns the juice into a protein-packed milkshake with a lusciously light and frothy topping. This really is quite a filling drink and is a great choice for those who feel that their life is too busy to prepare really nutritious food. A quick and easy drink that is good for you too – what could be better?

Makes 1 large glass

1 large pear
150g/5oz/1¼ cups green grapes
15ml/1 tbsp wheatgerm
60ml/4 tbsp soya yogurt
ice cubes

Cook's tip
If you would prefer to use a dairy yogurt rather than the soya variety, substitute with the type of your choice. It is better that you stick with a natural (plain) yogurt as plenty of fruity flavour is gained from the pear and the grapes. Look for the 0 per cent fat varieties.

1 Using a vegetable peeler, peel the pear and chop the flesh into large chunks of roughly the same size.

2 Push half the pear chunks through a juicer, followed by the grapes and then the remaining chunks of pear. Transfer the juice to a small jug (pitcher).

3 Add the wheatgerm to the yogurt and stir to mix throughly.

4 Pour into the pear and grape juice, whisking until it is light and frothy. Pour the milkshake over ice cubes and serve.

Opposite: Dairy-free deluxe (left) and Pear flair (right)

Orange and raspberry smoothie

This exquisite blend combines the sharp-sweet taste of raspberries and the refreshing fruitiness of oranges with smooth yogurt. It tastes like creamy, fruit heaven in a glass. Even better, it takes just minutes to prepare, making it perfect as a quick breakfast juice for people in a hurry or, indeed, as a refreshing drink at any other time of day.

1 Place the raspberries and yogurt in a blender or food processor and process for about 1 minute until the mixture is smooth and creamy.

2 Add the orange juice to the raspberry and yogurt mixture and process for another 30 seconds or until thoroughly combined. Pour into tall glasses and serve immediately.

Makes 2–3 glasses

250g/9oz/1⅓ cups raspberries, chilled

200ml/7fl oz/scant 1 cup natural (plain) yogurt, chilled

300ml/½ pint/1¼ cups freshly squeezed orange juice, chilled

Cook's tip
For a super-chilled version, use frozen raspberries instead of fresh. You may need to blend the raspberries and yogurt for a little longer to get a really smooth result.

Mango and lime lassi

Inspired by the classic Indian drink, this tangy, fruity blend is great for breakfast or as a delicious pick-me-up at any time of day. Soft, ripe mango blended with yogurt and sharp, zesty lime and lemon juice makes a wonderfully thick, cooling drink that's packed with energy. It can also be enjoyed as a mellow soother when you need to unwind.

Makes 2 tall glasses

1 mango
finely grated rind and juice of 1 lime
15ml/1 tbsp lemon juice
5–10ml/1–2 tsp caster (superfine) sugar
100ml/3½fl oz/scant ½ cup natural
   (plain) yogurt
mineral water
1 extra lime, halved, to serve

1 Peel the mango and cut the flesh from the stone (pit). Put the flesh into a blender or food processor and add the lime rind and juice.

2 Add the lemon juice, sugar and natural yogurt. Whizz until completely smooth, scraping down the sides of the bowl, if necessary. Stir in a little mineral water to thin it down.

3 Serve immediately, with half a lime on the side of each glass so that more juice can be squeezed in, if desired.

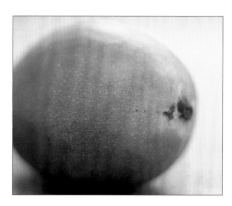

Peachy pleasure

When juiced together, apricots, peaches and kumquats produce the most amazingly vibrant orange-coloured juice with a flavour that has just as big a kick – and it is utterly delicious. The natural sugar content of apricots and peaches can vary enormously so you will need to add some honey to get the taste just right. Add a little at a time, then stir and, of course, keep tasting the juice until you find exactly the right flavour for you.

Makes 2 glasses

4 kumquats
6 ripe apricots, stoned (pitted)
2 peaches, stoned (pitted)
clear honey, to taste
ice cubes

Cook's tip
This drink is ideal for informal parties as well as a quick breakfast. If you are having friends round for dinner or drinks, make some funky New York cocktail-style stirrers. Simply halve some apricots, thread them on to long wooden skewers and place a skewer in each glass.

1 Using a small, sharp knife, roughly chop the kumquats and cut the apricots and peaches into large chunks. (There is no need to peel the fruit.)

2 Push the kumquat pieces through a juicer, followed by the apricot and peach chunks, alternating the fruit as you go to ensure they mix well.

3 Fill 2 large glasses with ice cubes and pour the fruit juice over the ice.

4 Stir in a little honey to the juice and taste. Add a little more honey if the juice is not sweet enough. (Be careful not to add too much honey, however, or it will overpower the other flavours and spoil the drink.) Serve immediately.

Tropicana

Even in winter this drink can brighten your day with its lively colour and deliciously tropical, fruity flavour. Any blend of tropical fruits will make a fabulous tasty juice as long as they are really ripe and ready for use. Persimmon and guavas can both be quite bitter if juiced when underripe so, if necessary, leave the fruits in the fruit bowl to ripen for a few days before using – the resulting juice will definitely be well worth the wait.

Makes 2–3 glasses

1 large papaya
1 persimmon
1 large guava
juice of 2 oranges
2 passion fruit, halved

Cook's tip
When chopping the fruit, cut some into chunky slices and reserve for decoration, if you like. Otherwise throw in some fruit chunks at the end to add some texture.

1 Halve the papaya, then scoop out and discard the black seeds. Using a small, sharp knife, cut the papaya, persimmon and guava flesh into large chunks of roughly the same size. (There's no need to peel them.)

2 Push the papaya through a juicer, followed by the persimmon and the guava. Pour the juice into a jug (pitcher), then add the orange juice and scoop in the passion fruit pulp. Whisk and chill until ready to serve.

Sweet dream

A soothing blend guaranteed to wake you up slowly, this fruity threesome is naturally sweet so there is no need for any additional sugar. Fresh grapefruit juice marries brilliantly with the dried fruits, and rich creamy yogurt makes a delicious contrast of colour and flavour – simply perfect to sip over a leisurely breakfast while reading the newspaper.

Makes 2 glasses

25g/1oz/scant ¼ cup dried figs or
   dates, stoned (pitted)
50g/2oz/¼ cup ready-to-eat prunes
25g/1oz/scant ¼ cup sultanas (golden raisins)
1 grapefruit
350ml/12fl oz/1½ cups full cream
   (whole) milk
30ml/2 tbsp Greek (US strained plain) yogurt

Cook's tip
For a dairy-free version of this drink, omit the yogurt and use soya or rice milk instead of ordinary milk. The consistency of the smoothie will not be as creamy but it will still be delicious – and perhaps better for those who prefer a lighter drink.

1 Put the dried fruits in a blender or food processor. Squeeze the grapefruit juice and add to the machine. Blend until smooth, scraping the mixture down from the side of the bowl, if necessary. Add the milk and blend until completely smooth.

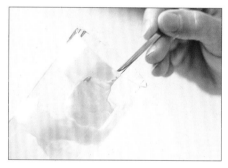

2 Using a teaspoon, tap a spoonful of the yogurt around the inside of each of two tall glasses. Pour in the fruit mixture and serve immediately.

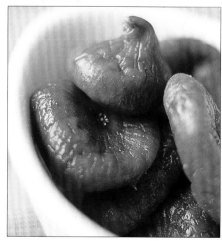

Raspberry and oatmeal smoothie

Just a spoonful or so of oatmeal gives substance to this tangy, invigorating drink. If you can, prepare it ahead of time because soaking the raw oats helps to break down the starch into natural sugars that are easy to digest. The smoothie will thicken up in the refrigerator so you might need to stir in a little extra juice or mineral water just before serving.

Makes 1 large glass

25ml/1½ tbsp medium oatmeal
150g/5oz/scant 1 cup raspberries
5–10ml/1–2 tsp clear honey
45ml/3 tbsp natural (plain) yogurt

1 Spoon the oatmeal into a heatproof bowl. Pour in 120ml/4fl oz/½ cup boiling water and leave to stand for about 10 minutes.

2 Put the soaked oats in a blender or food processor and add all but two or three of the raspberries, the honey and about 30ml/2 tbsp of the yogurt. Process until smooth, scraping down the side of the bowl if necessary.

Cook's tip

If you don't like raspberry pips (seeds) in your smoothies, press the fruit through a sieve with the back of a wooden spoon to make a smooth purée, then process with the oatmeal and yogurt as before. Alternatively, try using redcurrants instead of the raspberries.

Although a steaming bowl of porridge can't be beaten as a winter warmer, this smooth, oaty drink makes a great, light alternative in warmer months. It is a good way to make sure you get your fill of wholesome oats for breakfast.

3 Pour the raspberry and oatmeal smoothie into a large glass, swirl in the remaining yogurt and top with the reserved raspberries.

Big breakfast

Easy to prepare and even easier to drink, this energy-packed smoothie makes a great start to the day. Bananas and sesame seeds provide the perfect fuel in the form of slow-release carbohydrate that will keep you going all morning, while fresh and zesty orange juice and sweet, scented mango will set your tastebuds tingling first thing.

Makes 2 glasses

½ mango
1 banana
1 large orange
30ml/2 tbsp wheat bran
15ml/1 tbsp sesame seeds
10–15ml/2–3 tsp honey

Cook's tip
Mango juice is naturally very sweet so you may wish to add less honey or leave it out altogether. Taste the drink to decide how much you need.

1 Using a small, sharp knife, skin the mango, then slice the flesh off the stone (pit). Peel the banana and break it into short lengths, then place it in a blender or food processor with the mango.

2 Squeeze the juice from the orange and add to the blender or food processor along with the bran, sesame seeds and honey. Whizz until the mixture is smooth and creamy, then pour into glasses and serve.

Muesli smoothly

Another great breakfast booster, this store-cupboard smoothie can be a lifesaver if you've run out of fresh fruit. It's also a perfect option for breakfast in bed without the crumbs. Any extra drink can be covered and stored overnight in the refrigerator, although you'll probably need to add more milk in the morning as it will undoubtedly thicken on standing.

Makes 2 glasses

1 piece preserved stem ginger, plus
   30ml/2 tbsp syrup from the ginger jar
50g/2oz/¼ cup ready-to-eat dried apricots,
   halved or quartered
40g/1½oz/scant ½ cup natural
   muesli (granola)
about 200ml/7fl oz/scant 1 cup
   semi-skimmed (low-fat) milk

Cook's tip
Apricot and ginger are perfect partners in this divine drink. It makes an incredibly healthy, tasty breakfast, but is so delicious and indulgent that you could even serve it as a dessert after a summer meal.

1 Chop the preserved ginger and put it in a blender or food processor with the syrup, apricots, muesli and milk.

2 Process until smooth, adding more milk if necessary. Serve in wide glasses.

Late breakfast

This energizing blend is simply bursting with goodness, just what you need when the morning has got off to a slow start. Not only is tofu a perfect source of protein, it is also rich in minerals and contains nutrients that protect against dangerous diseases. Blended with seeds and vitamin-rich strawberries, this creamy blend should see you through until lunchtime. Store any leftovers in the refrigerator for later in the day or the following morning.

Makes 2 glasses

250g/9oz firm tofu
200g/7oz/1¾ cups strawberries
45ml/3 tbsp pumpkin or sunflower seeds,
   plus extra for sprinkling
30–45ml/2–3 tbsp clear honey
juice of 2 large oranges
juice of 1 lemon

Cook's tip
Almost any other fruit can be used instead of the strawberries. Those that blend well, such as mangoes, bananas, peaches, plums and raspberries, work particularly well as a substitute.

1 Roughly chop the tofu, then hull and roughly chop the strawberries. Reserve a few strawberry chunks.

2 Put all the ingredients in a blender or food processor and blend until completely smooth, scraping the mixture down from the side of the bowl, if necessary.

3 Pour into tumblers and sprinkle with extra seeds and strawberry chunks.

A good fix

While some people thrive on a glass of freshly juiced fruits first thing in the morning, others can't quite get going without their daily caffeine fix in the form of strong coffee. This gorgeous mocha smoothie combines decadent dark chocolate and caffeine-rich coffee in a deliciously frothy energizing mix. This is an intensely sweet and indulgent way to start the day – so don't treat yourself too often.

Makes 1 large glass

40g/1½oz plain (semisweet) chocolate,
    plus extra for decoration
5–10ml/1–2 tsp instant espresso powder
300ml/½ pint/1¼ cups full cream (whole) milk
30ml/2 tbsp double (heavy) cream (optional)
ice cubes
cocoa powder (unsweetened), for dusting

1 Chop the chocolate into pieces and place in a small, heavy pan with the espresso powder and 100ml/3½fl oz/ scant ½ cup of the milk. Heat very gently, stirring with a wooden spoon, until the chocolate has melted. Remove from the heat and pour into a bowl. Leave to cool for 10 minutes.

2 Add the remaining milk and cream, if using, and whisk the mixture together until smooth and frothy – you could use a handheld blender wand. Pour the smoothie over ice cubes in a large glass or mug and serve sprinkled with cocoa powder and chocolate shavings.

smooth
and
simple

Refreshingly tangy or as smooth as silk, super
smoothies have earned their place as one of our
favourite drinks. Keep them simple with pure fruit
blends, or try something a little different by adding
creamed coconut, fruit tea, herbs or spices. Let
the ideas in this irresistible chapter inspire you to
experiment with all kinds of combinations.

Ruby dreamer

Figs have a distinctive yet delicate taste and are best used in simple combinations, with ingredients that enhance, rather than mask, their flavour. Like most fruits, fresh figs are now available most of the year round but they are often at their best in winter when ruby oranges are also in season – giving you the perfect excuse to make this veritable treat of a smoothie.

1 Cut off the hard, woody tips from the stalks of the figs, then use a sharp knife to cut each fruit in half.

2 Squeeze the oranges, using a citrus juicer or by hand. Pour the juice into a blender or food processor and add the figs and sugar. Process well until the mixture is really smooth and fairly thick, scraping the fruit down from the side of the bowl, if necessary.

3 Add lemon juice and blend briefly. Pour over crushed ice and serve.

Makes 2 glasses

6 large ripe figs
4 ruby oranges
15ml/1 tbsp dark muscovado (molasses) sugar
30–45ml/2–3 tbsp lemon juice
crushed ice

Cook's tip
If you cannot find ruby oranges, use any other type of orange. The colour of the juice, however, will not be quite so vibrant.

Mango mania

Even people on a dairy-free diet can enjoy rich, creamy, indulgent drinks. This one is made using soya milk, which is particularly good in milkshakes and smoothies. It has a lovely caramel flavour that blends brilliantly with fruit purées, especially those made from fruits with an intense, naturally sweet taste like mangoes.

Makes 2 tall glasses

1 medium mango
300ml/½ pint/1¼ cups soya milk
finely grated rind and juice of 1 lime,
    plus extra rind for garnish
15–30ml/1–2 tbsp clear honey
crushed ice

Cook's tip
If you like very sweet drinks, choose soya milk sweetened with apple juice for this recipe. It is readily available in supermarkets and has a really rich flavour.

1 Using a sharp knife, peel the mango and cut the flesh off the stone (pit). Place the chopped flesh in a blender or food processor and add the soya milk, lime rind and juice and a little honey. Blend until smooth and frothy.

2 Taste the mixture and add more honey, if you like, blending until well mixed. Place some crushed ice in two glasses, then pour over the smoothie. Sprinkle with lime rind and serve.

Smooth and simple

Pre-packed and ready to use, a mixed bag of summer fruits (which can be bought from the freezer section in most large supermarkets) makes an unbelievably simple, fruity base for drinks. The frozen fruits mean that the final blend is perfectly chilled as well, so you don't need to add ice. Mixed with orange juice and enriched with a tempting swirl of cream, this smoothie is made in a flash – the perfect accompaniment to a relaxing afternoon in the sunshine.

Makes 3 glasses

500g/1lb 2oz frozen mixed summer fruits,
    partially thawed
30ml/2 tbsp caster (superfine) sugar
about 300ml/½ pint/1¼ cups freshly
    squeezed orange juice
60ml/4 tbsp single (light) cream

Cook's tip
If you do not want to squeeze the oranges, you can buy juice – but avoid the concentrated types.

1 Tip all but a few of the summer fruits into a blender or food processor and add the sugar and orange juice. Blend until smooth, adding a little more orange juice if the mixture is too thick.

2 Pour the smoothie into 3 tall glasses and, using a teaspoon, swirl a little cream into each glass. Top with the reserved fruits and serve with long spoons to mix in the cream.

Fruit-tea smoothie

Depending on your preference you can use any of the varied assortment of fruit teas, now readily available in most large supermarkets, for this thick, creamy blend. This recipe uses dried apricots and apples but you could easily replace these with dried pears, peaches or tropical dried fruits. From start to finish, this smoothie takes about one hour to prepare, so make sure you don't leave this one until the last minute.

Makes 2 glasses

50g/2oz dried apples
25g/1oz dried apricots
2 fruit teabags
juice of 1 lemon
30ml/2 tbsp crème fraîche or natural
    (plain) yogurt
mineral water (optional)

Cook's tip
Apple and lemon, apple and mango, forest berries and strawberry and raspberry fruit teas are just a few that are readily available. When choosing the dried fruit, pick the types that will work best with the flavours in your tea.

1 Using a small, sharp knife, roughly chop the dried apples and apricots. Steep the teabags in 300ml/½ pint/ 1¼ cups boiling water for 5 minutes, then remove the teabags.

2 Add the chopped fruit to the tea and leave to stand for 30 minutes. Chill in the refrigerator for about 30 minutes until the tea is completely cold.

3 Put the fruit and tea mixture into a blender or food processor and add the lemon juice. Blend well until smooth, scraping the mixture down from the side of the bowl, if necessary.

4 Add the crème fraîche or yogurt and blend briefly, adding a little mineral water if the smoothie is too thick. Serve in tall glasses.

Very berry

Fresh and frozen cranberries are often in short supply, but dried berries are available all year round and make a tasty dairy-free shake when combined with soya milk. Tiny crimson redcurrants make the perfect partner for the dried cranberries in this refreshingly tart, sparkling smoothie, and this low-fat blend is packed with natural sugars, essential nutrients and vitamins.

Makes 1 large glass

25g/1oz/¼ cup dried cranberries
150g/5oz/1¼ cups redcurrants, plus extra
  to decorate
10ml/2 tsp clear honey
50ml/2fl oz/¼ cup soya milk
sparkling mineral water

1 Put the cranberries in a small bowl, pour over 90ml/6 tbsp boiling water and leave to stand for 10 minutes.

2 String the redcurrants by drawing the stems through the tines of a fork to pull off the delicate currants.

3 Put the currants in a food processor or blender with the cranberries and soaking water. Blend well until smooth.

4 Add the honey and soya milk and whizz briefly to combine the ingredients.

5 Pour the berry shake into a large glass, then top with a little sparkling mineral water to lighten the drink. Drape the redcurrants decoratively over the edge of the glass and serve the smoothie immediately.

Cook's tip
Allowing time for the dried cranberries to rehydrate means they will become plump and juicy – making them much easier to blend and maximizing their flavour.

Purple haze

Thick, dark blueberry purée swirled into pale and creamy vanilla-flavoured buttermilk looks stunning and tastes simply divine. Despite its creaminess, the buttermilk gives this sumptuous smoothie a delicious sharp tang. If you do not like buttermilk or cannot find it in your local supermarket, you could use a mixture of half natural yogurt and half milk instead.

Makes 2 tall glasses

250g/9oz/2¼ cups blueberries
50g/2oz/¼ cup caster (superfine) sugar
15ml/1 tbsp lemon juice
300ml/½ pint/1¼ cups buttermilk
5ml/1 tsp vanilla essence (extract)
150ml/¼ pint/⅔ cup full cream (whole) milk

1 Push the blueberries through a juicer and stir in 15ml/1 tbsp of the sugar and the lemon juice. Stir well and divide between two tall glasses.

2 Put the buttermilk, vanilla essence, milk and remaining sugar in a blender or food processor and blend until really frothy. (Alternatively, use a hand-held electric blender and blend until the mixture froths up.)

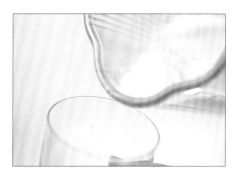

3 Pour the buttermilk mixture over the blueberry juice so the mixtures swirl together naturally – there is no need to stir them together as it tastes and looks better if they remain separate to a certain degree. Serve immediately.

Cook's tip
Deep violet blueberry juice makes a fantastic contrast in both colour and flavour to the buttermilk. If you cannot get hold of blueberries, other slightly tart fruits such as raspberries or blackberries would also work in this creamy combination.

Berry smooth

This simple recipe uses oat milk, a cholesterol-free, calcium-rich alternative to cow's milk, and a good partner to sweet summer fruits. Although a good store-cupboard stand-by, you might prefer to keep the oat milk in the refrigerator, ready for an impromptu milkshake whenever you're in the mood. For a really chilled, extremely refreshing flavour, use a mixed bag of semi-thawed frozen fruits, which will blend to a fabulously thick consistency.

Makes 2 glasses

250g/9oz frozen mixed summer fruits,
    partially thawed, plus extra to garnish
130g/4½oz/generous ½ cup soya yogurt
45ml/3 tbsp vanilla syrup
350ml/12fl oz/1½ cups oat milk

Cook's tip
Vanilla syrup is really sweet and full of flavour, great for giving drinks and desserts a deep, mellow flavour. If you cannot find any, use 45ml/3 tbsp caster (superfine) sugar and 5ml/1 tsp good quality vanilla essence (extract).

1 Put the partially thawed mixed summer fruits in a blender or food processor. Add the soya yogurt and blend thoroughly to make a thick purée. Scrape the mixture down from the side of the bowl with a rubber spatula, if necessary, and blend again, briefly, to incorporate into the mixture.

2 Add the vanilla syrup and oat milk to the fruit purée and blend the mixture again until smooth.

3 Transfer the smoothie to a small jug (pitcher) and chill, or pour it into two tall glasses and serve immediately, decorated with the extra fruits.

Pear, rhubarb and cranberry cooler

For best results this delicious smoothie should be made with really ripe and extremely juicy pears, so if the ones you buy are hard, leave them in the fruit bowl for several days before making this fresh and fruity treat. Do not forget to cook the rhubarb well in advance so that it has plenty of time to cool down before you start blending.

Makes 3–4 glasses

400g/14oz early rhubarb
2 large ripe pears
130g/4½oz/generous 1 cup fresh or
    frozen cranberries
90g/3½oz/½ cup caster (superfine) sugar
mineral water (optional)

Cook's tip
If you are using frozen cranberries, don't bother to thaw them first. They'll still blend, and their icy coolness will chill the smoothie to just the right temperature.

1 Using a small, sharp knife, trim the rhubarb and cut into 2cm/¾in lengths.

2 Place the rhubarb slices in a pan with 90ml/6 tbsp water and cover with a tight-fitting lid. Cook gently for about 5 minutes or until tender. Transfer to a bowl and leave to cool, putting several pieces aside for garnish.

3 Peel, quarter and core the pears and tip into a blender or food processor with the cranberries, the rhubarb and its cooking juices and the sugar.

4 Blend until smooth, scraping down the side of the bowl, if necessary. Thin with mineral water, if you like, then serve, garnished with the rhubarb pieces.

Rosemary nectar

This is one of those smoothies that's only worth making if you've got the perfect, ripe ingredients. The fabulously aromatic fragrance of fresh rosemary reacts with the sweet, scented flavour of juicy nectarines to produce a delicious blend with a mouthwatering taste that will almost explode on your tongue – make plenty as you're sure to want more.

Makes 3 glasses

4 long rosemary sprigs, plus extra
   to decorate
15ml/1 tbsp golden caster (superfine) sugar
2.5ml/½ tsp ground ginger
2 oranges
4 nectarines
ice cubes

1 Put the rosemary sprigs in a small pan with the sugar, ground ginger and 150ml/¼ pint/⅔ cup water. Heat gently until the sugar dissolves, then simmer for 1 minute. Remove from the heat, transfer the sprigs and syrup to a bowl and leave to cool.

2 Squeeze the oranges. Halve and stone (pit) the nectarines and put in a food processor or blender with the orange juice. Process until smooth but don't worry if there are a few specks of nectarine skin dotting the juice.

3 Remove the rosemary from the syrup and pour into the juice. Blend briefly.

4 Put a few ice cubes in each glass and fill with the juice. Serve immediately, with extra rosemary sprigs to decorate.

Cook's tip
If you've bought nectarines only to find that they're as hard as bullets, leave them in the fruit bowl for a couple of days – they should ripen fairly quickly.

Vanilla snow

While a good quality vanilla essence is perfectly acceptable for flavouring drinks, a far more aromatic taste will be achieved using a vanilla pod. This simple smoothie is deliciously scented, creamy and thick, and well worth the extravagance of using a whole vanilla pod. Its lovely, snowy whiteness is delightfully speckled with tiny black vanilla seeds.

Makes 3 glasses

1 vanilla pod (bean)
25g/1oz/2 tbsp caster (superfine) sugar
3 eating apples
300g/11oz/1⅓ cups natural (plain) yogurt

1 Using the tip of a sharp knife, split open the vanilla pod lengthways. Put it in a small pan with the sugar and 75ml/5 tbsp water. Heat until the sugar dissolves, then boil for 1 minute. Remove from the heat and leave to steep for 10 minutes.

2 Cut the apples into large chunks and push through the juicer, then pour the juice into a large bowl or jug (pitcher).

3 Lift the vanilla pod out of the pan and scrape the tiny black seeds back into the syrup. Pour into the apple juice.

4 Add the yogurt to the bowl or jug and whisk well by hand or with an electric mixer until the smoothie is thick and frothy. Pour into glasses and serve.

Cook's tip
Like most smoothies, this one should ideally be served well chilled. Either use apples and yogurt straight from the refrigerator, or chill briefly before serving. To make a thick, icy version, you could try using frozen yogurt.

Raspberry, apple and rose water smoothie

Although usually put through the juicer for drinking, apples can be blended as long as you process them well to ensure a really flavour-packed smoothie. This recipe is thinned with fresh apple juice, which can be either shop-bought (make sure it is good quality) or home-made.

Makes 2 glasses

2 eating apples
10ml/2 tsp caster (superfine) sugar
15ml/1 tbsp lemon juice
130g/4½oz/¾ cup fresh or frozen raspberries
150ml/¼ pint/⅔ cup apple juice
15–30ml/1–2 tbsp rose water
whole raspberries and rose petals,
　to decorate (optional)

Cook's tip

If you prefer raspberries without the pips (seeds), blend them first and then push the purée through a sieve to remove the pips before mixing it with the apples.

1 Peel and core the apples and put in a blender or food processor with the sugar and lemon juice. Blend well until smooth, scraping the mixture down from the side of the bowl, if necessary.

2 Add the raspberries and apple juice to the apple purée and blend until completely smooth.

3 Add the rose water to the smoothie and blend briefly to combine.

4 Pour the smoothie into two medium glasses and place whole raspberries and rose petals on top of the drinks to decorate, if you like. Serve the smoothie immediately, or chill in the refrigerator until ready to serve.

Coconut and hazelnut smoothie

This intensely nutty, rich and creamy drink is one to sip at your leisure. Leftovers can be put in the refrigerator for up to a couple of days, in which time the flavour of the hazelnuts will develop.

Makes 2 glasses

90g/3½oz/scant 1 cup whole
　blanched hazelnuts
25g/1oz/2 tbsp golden caster
　(superfine) sugar
2.5ml/½ tsp almond essence (extract)
200ml/7fl oz/scant 1 cup coconut cream
30ml/2 tbsp double (heavy) cream (optional)
150ml/¼ pint/⅔ cup mineral water
crushed ice

Cook's tip

If you want a frothy topping on this creamy smoothie, whisk it using a handheld electric wand after adding the mineral water, before pouring into the glasses.

1 Roughly chop the hazelnuts and lightly toast them in a small frying pan, turning frequently. Leave to cool, then tip the nuts into a blender or food processor with the caster sugar and blend well until very finely ground.

2 Add the almond essence, coconut cream and double cream, if using, and blend thoroughly until smooth.

3 Strain the mixture through a sieve into a jug (pitcher), pressing the pulp down with the back of a spoon to extract as much juice as possible. Stir in the mineral water.

4 Half-fill two glasses with crushed ice and pour over the nut smoothie. Serve the drinks immediately, or chill in the refrigerator until ready to serve.

Cinnamon squash

Lightly cooked butternut squash makes a delicious smoothie. It has a wonderfully rich, rounded flavour that is lifted perfectly by the addition of tart citrus juice and warm, spicy cinnamon. Imagine pumpkin pie as a gorgeous smooth drink and you're halfway to experiencing the flavours of this lusciously sweet and tantalizing treat.

2 Put the cooled squash in a blender or food processor and add the ground cinnamon.

3 Squeeze the lemons and grapefruit and pour the juice over the squash, then add the muscovado sugar.

4 Process the ingredients until they are very smooth. If necessary, pause to scrape down the side of the food processor or blender.

5 Put a few ice cubes in two or three short glasses and pour over the smoothie. Serve immediately.

Makes 2–3 glasses

1 small butternut squash,
    about 600g/1lb 6oz
2.5ml/½ tsp ground cinnamon
3 large lemons
1 grapefruit
60ml/4 tbsp light muscovado (brown) sugar
ice cubes

Cook's tip
If you can only buy a large squash, cook it all and add the leftovers to stew or soup.

1 Halve the squash, scoop out and discard the seeds and cut the flesh into chunks. Cut away the skin and discard. Steam or boil the squash for 10–15 minutes until just tender. Drain well and leave to stand until cool.

Green devil

Choose a well-flavoured avocado, such as a knobbly, dark-skinned Haas, for this slightly spicy, hot and sour smoothie. Cucumber adds a refreshing edge, while lemon and lime juice zip up the flavour, and the chilli sauce adds an irresistible fiery bite. This is one little devil that is sure to liven up even the most lethargic days.

Makes 2–3 glasses

1 small ripe avocado
½ cucumber
30ml/2 tbsp lemon juice
30ml/2 tbsp lime juice
10ml/2 tsp caster (superfine) sugar
pinch of salt
250ml/8fl oz/1 cup apple juice or
    mineral water
10–20ml/2–4 tsp sweet chilli sauce
ice cubes
red chilli curls, to decorate

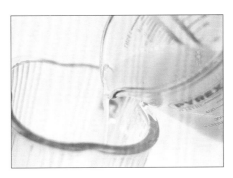

1 Halve the avocado and use a sharp knife to remove the stone (pit). Scoop the flesh from both halves into a blender or food processor. Peel and roughly chop the cucumber and add to the blender or food processor, then add the lemon and lime juice, the caster sugar and a little salt.

2 Process the ingredients until smooth and creamy, then add the apple juice or mineral water and a little of the chilli sauce. Blend once more to lightly mix the ingredients together.

3 Pour the smoothie over ice cubes. Decorate with red chilli curls and serve with stirrers and extra chilli sauce.

Cook's tip
To make chilli curls, core and seed a fresh red chilli and cut it into very fine strips. Put the strips in a bowl of iced water and leave to stand for 20 minutes or until the strips curl. Use them to decorate this smoothie.

Seductively smooth avocados are as good for you as they taste. Their fresh vitamin- and mineral-rich flesh is reputed to be fantastic for healthy hair and skin.

cool
creamy
shakes

Milkshakes can be either refreshing and fruity or smooth and creamy, but they are always a treat. Inspiring ingredients include brownies and garden mint, and there are several shakes made with more traditional flavours such as vanilla or banana. Fun for kids and nostalgically appealing for adults, comfort drinks never looked or tasted so good.

Real vanilla milkshake

This is a milkshake for connoisseurs: it is the cream of the crop and definitely one to linger over. Nothing beats the flavour achieved by infusing a vanilla pod in the milk beforehand, but if you just cannot wait for the milk to cool, use a teaspoon of good quality vanilla essence instead.

Makes 2 glasses

1 vanilla pod (bean)
400ml/14fl oz/1⅔ cups full cream
  (whole) milk
200ml/7fl oz/scant 1 cup single (light) cream
4 scoops vanilla ice cream

1 Using a sharp knife, score the vanilla pod down the centre. Place in a small pan, pour the milk over and bring slowly to the boil.

2 Remove the pan from the heat but leave the pod in the milk. Leave to stand until the milk has cooled.

3 Remove the vanilla pod from the cooled milk and scrape out the seeds with the tip of a knife. Put the seeds in a blender or food processor with the milk and cream. Blend until combined.

4 Add the vanilla ice cream to the mixture and blend well until it is deliciously thick and frothy. Pour the smoothie into two large glasses and serve immediately with stirrers and straws to decorate, if you like.

Cook's tip
This classic milkshake is extremely rich and creamy, but if you'd prefer a lighter consistency, replace half the cream with the same quantity of extra milk.

Simply strawberry

Nothing evokes a sense of summer wellbeing more than the scent and flavour of sweet, juicy strawberries. This recipe uses an abundance of these fragrant fruits so, if possible, make it when the season is right and local ones are at their most plentiful.

Makes 2 glasses

400g/14oz/3½ cups strawberries, plus extra
   to decorate
30–45ml/2–3 tbsp icing (confectioners') sugar
200g/7oz/scant 1 cup Greek (US strained
   plain) yogurt
60ml/4 tbsp single (light) cream

Cook's tip
You can replace the strawberries with other fruits if they are not in season. Try using fresh bananas instead to make another very popular milkshake.

1 Hull the strawberries and place them in a blender or food processor with 30ml/2 tbsp of the icing sugar. Blend to a smooth purée, scraping the mixture down from the side of the bowl with a rubber spatula, if necessary.

2 Add the yogurt and cream and blend again until smooth and frothy. Check the sweetness, adding a little more sugar if you find the flavour too sharp. Pour into glasses and serve decorated with extra strawberries.

Rose petal and almond milk

If you're lucky enough to have a mass of roses in the garden, it's well worth sacrificing a few to make this delicately scented summer smoothie. Thickened and flavoured with ground ratafia biscuits, this fragrant drink is the perfect way to relax on a hot lazy afternoon.

Makes 2 glasses

15g/½oz scented rose petals (preferably
    pink), plus extra to decorate
300ml/½ pint/1¼ cups milk
25g/1oz ratafia biscuits (almond macaroons)
ice cubes

Cook's tip

If you have bought roses, or even if you have picked them from your own garden, make sure you wash the petals thoroughly before you use them for cooking. This will help to remove any chemicals or pesticides that may have been sprayed on to the flowers.

1 Put the rose petals in a small pan with half the milk and bring just to the boil. Put the ratafia biscuits in a bowl, pour over the hot milk and leave to stand for 10 minutes.

2 Transfer the mixture to a blender or food processor with the remaining milk, and blend until smooth.

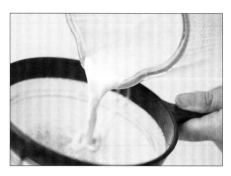

3 Strain the milk through a sieve into a wide jug (pitcher) to remove any lumps of biscuit or rose petals that have not been blended properly, and chill for at least 1 hour.

4 When the milk is well chilled, pour over ice cubes and serve immediately, decorating with rose petals, if you like.

Banana and maple crunch

Brilliant for making quick and easy blended drinks, bananas have a natural affinity with maple syrup and pecan nuts – what a combination. Serve this creamy, syrupy smoothie over ice and, if you are feeling decadent, dunk in some chunky chocolate cookies to scoop up a mouthful. It is best to serve this smoothie as soon as it is ready because it will not keep well. Finishing it off in one sitting should not be too difficult.

Makes 2 glasses

2 large bananas
50g/2oz/½ cup pecan nuts, plus extra to serve
150ml/¼ pint/⅔ cup full cream (whole) milk
60ml/4 tbsp pure maple syrup
crushed ice

Cook's tips

It is important to use ripe bananas in this recipe and, although you could replace the nuts with another variety such as hazelnuts, the combination of pecans, bananas and maple syrup is such a classic that any variation won't be as good.

1 Put the bananas in a blender or food processor and process until smooth. Add the nuts and blend again until thoroughly combined.

2 The nuts must be finely ground so stop and scrape down the side of the bowl once or twice, if necessary.

3 Add the maple syrup, then pour the milk over the banana paste and blend again until creamy.

4 Half-fill two large glasses with crushed ice and pour the smoothie over the top. Serve sprinkled with extra pecan nuts, if you like.

Honey and banana milkshake

This delicious drink demonstrates just how smooth and creamy a milkshake can be, even without using dairy produce. Make it using either soya or rice milk together with a vanilla-flavoured, iced non-dairy dessert to achieve a surprisingly rich and creamy flavour. Bananas make a nutritious, energy-boosting addition to drinks – this one is almost a meal in itself.

Makes 2 glasses

2 bananas
30ml/2 tbsp clear honey
15ml/1 tbsp lemon juice
300ml/½ pint/1¼ cups soya or rice milk
4 scoops vanilla iced non-dairy dessert

Cook's tip
If you are happy to use dairy produce, simply use ordinary milk and vanilla ice cream in place of the non-dairy ingredients.

1 Break the bananas into pieces and put in a blender or food processor with the honey and lemon juice. Blend until very smooth, scraping the mixture down from the side of the bowl with a rubber spatula, if necessary.

2 Add the soya or rice milk and two scoops of iced non-dairy dessert, then blend until smooth. Pour into tall glasses and add another scoop of dessert to each. Serve immediately.

Stem ginger and pear shake

Although fresh fruit cannot be beaten for its flavour and nutritional value, canned varieties are a good store-cupboard stand-by for when you've run out of fresh. They are still nutritionally sound, particularly if packed in natural, unsweetened fruit juice. Preserved stem ginger makes the perfect partner to pears in this taste-tingling, creamy creation.

1 Shave off some wafer-thin slices from one of the pieces of ginger and reserve. Roughly chop the remaining ginger. Drain the pears, reserving about 150ml/¼ pint/⅔ cup of the juice.

2 Put the pears, measured juice and chopped ginger in a blender or food processor and blend until smooth, scraping the mixture down from the side of the bowl, if necessary.

3 Strain through a sieve into a jug (pitcher). Whisk in the milk, cream and ginger syrup and pour into two glasses. Serve scattered with the ginger shavings.

Makes 2 glasses

3 pieces (about 65g/2½oz) preserved stem
   ginger, plus 30ml/2 tbsp ginger syrup from
   the jar
400g/14oz can pears in natural fruit juice
150ml/¼ pint/⅔ cup full cream (whole) milk
100ml/3½fl oz/scant ½ cup single
   (light) cream
ice cubes

Cook's tip
If you like your milkshake really smooth, strain the pear mixture through a sieve to remove any bits of fibre that might remain in the pears. However, if you like the consistency of the stringy bits, skip this part of the recipe.

Lemon meringue

Just as lemon meringue pie is a favourite dessert, this wonderful milkshake is sure to become a favourite drink. The blend of sweet meringue and lemon is carefully balanced in a velvety smooth, ice-cool drink that is not too rich and surprisingly refreshing. This really is a dessert in a glass and will undoubtedly go down well at your next dinner party.

2 Coarsely crush 15g/½oz of the meringues and reserve for decoration. Break the remainder into a blender or food processor. Add the lemon syrup and blend until smooth.

3 With the machine still running, gradually pour in the milk until the mixture is pale and frothy. Add the ice cream and blend again until smooth.

4 Pour the milkshake into tall glasses and decorate the sides with lemon slices or twists of lemon peel. Scatter the reserved meringue on top and serve immediately with spoons.

Makes 2 glasses

30ml/2 tbsp caster (superfine) sugar
3 lemons
50g/2oz crisp white meringues
300ml/½ pint/¼ cups full cream (whole) milk
2 scoops vanilla ice cream
lemon slices or twists of peel,
  to decorate

Cook's tip
When shopping for the lemons to decorate this drink, be sure to buy the unwaxed variety.

1 Put the sugar in a small pan with 100ml/3½fl oz/scant ½ cup water and heat gently until the sugar dissolves. Pour into a jug (pitcher). Squeeze the lemons using a citrus juicer and add the juice to the syrup. Leave to cool.

Garden mint milkshake

If you have mint growing in your garden, pick some for this recipe, as the fresher the mint, the better the flavour will be. The mint is infused in a sugar syrup, then left to cool before being blended to an aromatic, frothy shake with yogurt and creamy milk. The final milkshake is speckled with tiny green flecks, but if you prefer a completely smooth texture, you can strain these out.

Makes 2 tall glasses

25g/1oz/1 cup fresh mint
50g/2oz/¼ cup caster (superfine) sugar
200g/7oz/scant 1 cup natural
    (plain) yogurt
200ml/7fl oz/scant 1 cup full cream
    (whole) milk
15ml/1 tbsp lemon juice
crushed ice cubes
icing (confectioners') sugar, to decorate

2 Heat the mixture, stirring occasionally, until the sugar dissolves, then boil for 2 minutes. Remove the pan from the heat and set aside until the syrup is completely cool.

3 Strain the cooled syrup through a sieve into a jug (pitcher), pressing the mint against the side of the sieve with the back of a spoon. Pour into a blender or food processor.

4 Add the yogurt and milk to the syrup and blend until smooth and frothy. Add two of the reserved mint sprigs and the lemon juice and blend until the milkshake is specked with tiny green flecks.

5 Put the crushed ice in tall glasses or tumblers and pour over the milkshake. Dust the mint sprigs with icing sugar and use to decorate the glasses. Serve.

1 Pull out four small mint sprigs and set aside. Roughly snip the remaining leaves into a small pan. Add the sugar and pour over 105ml/7 tbsp water.

Rosemary and almond cream

This delightful concoction is definitely one to choose if you are looking for something a little different. Fresh sprigs of rosemary, infused in milk, provide a gentle fragrance and flavour that blends deliciously with the sweet ratafia biscuits. Frothed up with creamy, melting vanilla ice cream, this velvety smooth creation is quite simply superb.

Makes 2 glasses

4 long sprigs of fresh rosemary
400ml/14fl oz/1⅔ cups full cream (whole) milk
50g/2oz ratafia biscuits (almond macaroons) or amaretti, plus extra to decorate
3 large scoops vanilla ice cream
frosted rosemary sprigs, to decorate

Cook's tip
To make frosted rosemary sprigs, lightly coat the sprigs in a little beaten egg white. Dip in caster (superfine) sugar and leave to dry.

1 Put the rosemary sprigs in a small pan. Add 150ml/¼ pint/⅔ cup of the milk and heat very gently until the milk begins to boil. Remove the pan from the heat and tip the mixture into a bowl. Leave to cool for 10 minutes.

2 Remove the rosemary sprigs and carefully pour the still warm milk into a blender or food processor. Add the ratafia biscuits and blend until smooth and creamy. Add the remaining 250ml/8fl oz/1 cup milk and blend the mixture thoroughly.

3 Scoop the vanilla ice cream into the milk and biscuit mixture and blend until it is fully incorporated. Pour into large glasses and serve the milkshake immediately, decorating the top of each glass with delicate frosted rosemary sprigs and a few pieces of crumbled ratafia biscuits.

Pistachio thick-shake

Don't be put off by the presence of rice in this lovely, layered dairy-free milkshake. Blended with soya milk, pistachio nuts and non-dairy ice cream, it makes a dreamy, creamy blend that can be sipped, layer by layer, or swirled together with a pretty stirrer. As its name suggests, this shake is wonderfully rich and decadent; serve it in tall narrow glasses.

Makes 3–4 small glasses

550ml/18fl oz/2½ cups soya milk
50g/2oz/generous ¼ cup pudding rice
60ml/4 tbsp caster (superfine) sugar
finely grated rind of 1 lemon
75g/3oz/¾ cup shelled pistachio nuts, plus extra to decorate
300ml/10fl oz vanilla iced non-dairy dessert
5ml/1 tsp almond essence (extract)

1 Put the soya milk in a large, heavy pan with the rice, sugar and lemon rind. Bring slowly to the boil, then reduce the heat to simmer. Partially cover the pan with a lid and cook on the lowest heat for about 30 minutes, or until the rice is completely tender.

2 Transfer the rice to a heatproof bowl and leave to stand until completely cold.

3 Put the pistachio nuts in another heatproof bowl and cover with boiling water. Leave to stand for about 2 minutes and then drain.

4 Rub the pistachio nuts between several layers of kitchen paper to loosen the skins, then peel them away. (Don't worry about removing every bit of skin, but getting most of it off will make a prettier coloured milkshake.)

5 Tip the cold rice into a blender or food processor and blend until smooth. Put half the mixture in a bowl. Add the non-dairy dessert to the blender and blend until smooth. Pour into a separate bowl. Add the nuts, the reserved rice and the almond essence to the blender and process until the nuts are finely ground.

6 Layer the two mixtures in glasses and serve decorated with extra pistachios.

Marzipan and orange crush

The wintry scents and flavours of juicy oranges and marzipan make an interesting combination and the citrus juice adds a delicious refreshing tang to an otherwise very rich, creamy drink. It's a great blend to make if you are entertaining friends as its unusual blend of ingredients is sure to be a talking point. Make plenty of this irresistible shake and chill whatever you don't use in the refrigerator for another time.

Makes 3–4 glasses

130g/4½oz marzipan
finely grated rind and juice of 2 large oranges
juice of 1 lemon
150ml/¼ pint/⅔ cup mineral water
150ml/¼ pint/⅔ cup single (light) cream
ice cubes
orange wedges, to decorate (optional)

Cook's tip
Give this drink a whisk before serving, as it may have settled.

1 Break the marzipan into small pieces and put in a blender or food processor. Add the orange rind and juice along with the lemon juice. Blend the mixture thoroughly until smooth.

2 Add the mineral water and cream and blend again until smooth and frothy. Pour over ice cubes in glasses and serve decorated with the orange wedges, if you like.

Cherry and coconut shake

The season for fresh cherries is all too short, but canned cherries make a very good and surprisingly delicious stand-by. Here they are combined in a classic partnership with creamy coconut milk to make a rich, fruity drink that is perfect for people who are not too keen on really sweet, thick milkshakes. Make sure you buy pitted cherries, otherwise you will have to carefully stone them yourself before tipping them into the blender.

Makes 2 glasses

425g/15oz can pitted black cherries
  in syrup
200ml/7fl oz/scant 1 cup coconut milk
15ml/1 tbsp light muscovado (brown) sugar
150ml/¼ pint/⅔ cup black cherry-flavour
  yogurt
100ml/3½fl oz/scant ½ cup double
  (heavy) cream
lightly toasted shredded coconut,
  to decorate

Cook's tip
If you can't get black cherry flavour yogurt, use a vanilla or natural (plain) yogurt instead and add a little extra sugar when blending.

1 Tip the canned cherries into a sieve over a bowl to drain. Reserve the syrup for later.

2 Put the drained cherries in a blender or food processor with the coconut milk and sugar and blend briefly until fairly smooth. (Do not be tempted to over-blend the mixture or it may begin to separate.)

3 Pour the mixture through a sieve into a jug (pitcher), pressing the pulp down into the sieve with the back of a spoon to extract as much juice as possible.

4 Add the reserved cherry syrup, yogurt and cream and whisk lightly until smooth and frothy. Pour into glasses and scatter with shredded coconut.

Passionata

The combination of ripe passion fruit with sweet caramel is gorgeous in this dreamy milkshake. For convenience, you can easily make the caramel syrup and combine it with the fresh passion fruit juice in advance, so it's all ready for blending with the milk. For the best results make sure you use really ripe, crinkly passion fruit.

Makes 4 glasses

90g/3½oz/½ cup caster (superfine) sugar
juice of 2 large oranges
juice of 1 lemon
6 ripe passion fruit, plus extra for garnish
550ml/18fl oz/2½ cups full cream
   (whole) milk
ice cubes

1 Put the sugar in a small, heavy pan with 200ml/7fl oz/scant 1 cup water. Heat gently, stirring with a wooden spoon until the sugar has dissolved.

2 Bring the mixture to the boil and cook, without stirring, for about 5 minutes until the syrup has turned to a deep golden caramel. Watch closely towards the end of the cooking time as caramel can burn very quickly. If this happens, let the caramel cool, then throw it away and start again.

3 When the caramel has turned deep golden, immediately lower the base of the pan into cold water to prevent it from cooking any further.

4 Carefully add the orange and lemon juice, standing back slightly as the mixture will splutter. Return the pan to the heat and cook gently, stirring continuously, to make a smooth syrup. Transfer the syrup to a small heatproof bowl and set aside until it has cooled completely.

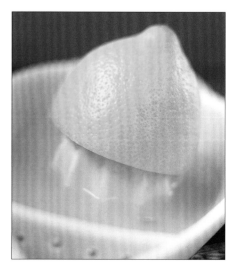

5 Halve the passion fruit and scoop the seeds into a blender or food processor. Add the caramel and milk and blend until smooth and frothy. Pour over ice and serve with a passion fruit garnish.

Rocky river

This rich, sweet milkshake combines chilled custard with decadent chocolate, chunky nuts and delicious marshmallows. It is great fun to make with children, who will enjoy its sticky, indulgent sweetness almost as much as the adults. Prepare this shake whenever you're really in need of a treat or when relaxing in the garden on a hot afternoon.

Makes 3 glasses

75g/3oz plain (semisweet) chocolate
40g/1½oz/scant ½ cup blanched almonds
50g/2oz pink and white marshmallows
600ml/1 pint/2½ cups good quality
   ready-made custard
300ml/½ pint/1¼ cups milk
30ml/2 tbsp caster (superfine) sugar
5ml/1 tsp vanilla essence (extract)

1 Coarsely grate the chocolate. Lightly toast the almonds, then chop them. Cut the marshmallows roughly into pieces, using scissors, reserving a few pieces for decoration.

2 Tip the custard into a blender or food processor and add the milk, sugar and vanilla essence. Blend briefly to combine.

3 Reserve a little chocolate for sprinkling, then add the remainder to the blender with the almonds and marshmallows. Blend until the marshmallows are chopped into small pieces.

4 Pour into big glasses and serve immediately, sprinkled with the reserved marshmallows and grated chocolate.

Cook's tip
Very cold chocolate can be difficult to grate. You might find it easier if you microwave it, very briefly, as this will make the chocolate less brittle for grating.

Cinnamon iced coffee

When the weather warms up, swap mugs of hot coffee for this treat of a summer cooler. Lightly flavoured with cinnamon and served icy cold, it's a smooth relaxing drink for when you need to unwind – and it's well worth keeping a jug in the refrigerator.

Makes 2 large glasses

5ml/1 tsp ground cinnamon
400ml/14fl oz/1⅔ cups full cream (whole) milk
40g/1½oz/3 tbsp caster (superfine) sugar
300ml/½ pint/1¼ cups strong cold espresso coffee
ice cubes
cinnamon sticks, to serve

Cook's tip
For a dinner party, why not spice things up and serve these shakes with a large dash of Bailey's or Tia Maria. These types of alcohol work particularly well with this drink's creaminess and its subtle cinnamon tones.

1 Put the cinnamon and 100ml/3½fl oz/ scant ½ cup of the milk in a small pan with the sugar. Bring the milk slowly to the boil then remove from the heat and leave to cool.

2 Turn the cinnamon milk into a large jug (pitcher) or bowl. Add the remaining milk and the coffee and whisk well, using a hand-held electric wand, until frothy. Pour into glasses with ice and serve with cinnamon sticks for stirrers.

Chocolate brownie milkshake

For a truly indulgent flavour, use home-made chocolate brownies in this fabulously tasty milkshake. It is very rich – and incredibly decadent – so sit back, relax and just enjoy a totally luxurious moment on your own – well, you wouldn't want to share it.

1 Crumble the chocolate brownies into a blender or food processor and add the milk. Blend until the mixture is a pale chocolate colour.

2 Add the ice cream and blend until smooth and frothy. Pour into a tall glass and spoon over a little whipped cream. Serve scattered with chocolate shavings or a dusting of cocoa powder.

Makes 1 large glass

40g/1½oz chocolate brownies
200ml/7fl oz/scant 1 cup full cream
    (whole) milk
2 scoops vanilla ice cream
a little whipped cream
chocolate shavings or cocoa powder
    (unsweetened), to decorate

Cook's tip
If you fancy treating yourself to a milkshake that's even more chocolatey than this one, replace the vanilla ice cream with the same amount of a chocolate or chocolate-chip variety.

drinks
for
kids

Drinks for breakfast, after school or even kids'
parties are transformed with these delicious
concoctions. There are fresh fruit squashes, fun
fizzes and shakes, and some real teatime treats
that could quite easily take the place of an ordinary
dessert or pudding. Let the kids help prepare them
and they'll enjoy these blends even more.

Fresh orange squash

Pushing oranges through a juicer rather than squeezing out the juice means you maximize the fruits' goodness and reduce the amount of wastage. Although this squash uses a significant amount of sugar in the syrup, at least you can rest assured that there are no secret colourings, flavourings and preservatives, making it a far healthier alternative to shop-bought versions – perfect for children who get through gallons of squash every day.

Makes about 550ml/18fl oz/2½ cups,
before diluting

90g/3½oz/½ cup caster (superfine) sugar
6 large oranges
still or sparkling mineral water, to serve

1 Put the sugar in a small, heavy pan with 100ml/3½fl oz/scant ½ cup water. Heat gently, stirring until the sugar has dissolved. Bring to the boil and boil rapidly for 3 minutes until the mixture is syrupy. Remove from the heat.

2 Cut away the skins from three of the oranges and chop the flesh into pieces small enough to fit through a juicer funnel. Chop the remaining oranges, with skins on, into similar-size pieces.

3 Push the orange pieces through the juicer, then mix with the sugar syrup. Pour into a bottle or jug (pitcher) and store in the refrigerator. To serve, dilute the orange squash to taste with still or sparkling mineral water.

Ruby red lemonade

Use blackberries or blueberries, or a mixture of the two, in this quick and easy fruit cordial.
A far healthier alternative to ready-made drinks, it's made in minutes and can be kept in the
refrigerator for several days. If you have a glut of summer fruits, it makes sense to prepare extra
and freeze it, preferably in single portions in ice-cube trays, so that children can easily pick
them out, then all they need do is drop them into a glass and top up with water.

3 Put the sugar in a small, heavy pan
with 100ml/3½fl oz/scant ½ cup water.
Heat gently until the sugar dissolves,
stirring with a wooden spoon, then
bring to the boil and boil for 3 minutes
until syrupy. Reserve until cool.

4 Mix the fruit juice with the syrup in a
jug (pitcher). For each serving pour
about 50ml/2fl oz/¼ cup fruit syrup into
a tumbler and add ice. Serve topped
up with sparkling mineral water.

**Makes about 350ml/12fl oz/1½ cups,
before diluting**

350g/12oz/3 cups blackberries or blueberries
130g/4½oz/scant ¾ cup golden caster
 (superfine) sugar
ice cubes
sparkling mineral water, to serve

1 Examine the blackberries or
blueberries carefully, removing any
tough stalks or leaves from the fruit,
and then wash them thoroughly. Allow
the fruit to dry.

2 Push handfuls of the fruit through
a juicer.

Strawberry and apple slush

Sweet, juicy strawberries make wonderfully fragrant juices, especially when they are grown outside in the summer. The juice has an almost perfect consistency that's not too thick and not too thin. The addition of apple juice and just a hint of vanilla creates a tantalizing, fruity treat that's ideal for children spending a lazy summer afternoon in the garden.

1 Pick out a couple of the prettiest strawberries and reserve for the decoration. Hull the remaining strawberries and roughly chop the apples into large chunks.

2 Push the fruits through a juicer and stir in the vanilla syrup.

3 Half-fill two tall glasses with ice. Add straws or stirrers and pour over the juice. Decorate with the reserved strawberries (slicing them, if you like) and serve immediately.

Makes 2 tall glasses

300g/11oz/2½ cups ripe strawberries
2 small, crisp eating apples
10ml/2 tsp vanilla syrup
crushed ice

Cook's tip
Vanilla syrup can be bought in jars from supermarkets and delicatessens. As an alternative, you could add a few drops of vanilla essence (extract) and a sprinkling of sugar, if necessary.

Lemon float

Old-fashioned lemonade made with freshly squeezed lemons is a far cry from the carbonated, synthetic commercial varieties. Served with generous scoops of ice cream and soda water, it makes the ultimate refreshing dessert drink. The lemonade can be stored in the refrigerator for up to two weeks, so it is well worth making a double batch.

Makes 4 large glasses

6 lemons, plus wafer-thin lemon slices,
   to decorate
200g/7oz/1 cup caster (superfine) sugar
8 scoops vanilla ice cream
soda water (club soda)

1 Finely grate the rind from the lemons, then squeeze out the juice using a citrus juicer or by hand.

2 Put the rind in a bowl with the sugar and pour over 600ml/1 pint/2½ cups boiling water. Stir until the sugar dissolves, then leave to cool.

3 Stir in the lemon juice. Strain into a jug (pitcher) and chill for several hours.

4 Put a scoop of the vanilla ice cream in each of the glasses, then half-fill with the lemonade and add plenty of lemon slices to decorate. Top up each glass with soda water, add another scoop of ice cream to each one and serve immediately with long-handled spoons.

Puppy love

Rather like bought slushy drinks, this sweet, semi-frozen fruit treat will be enjoyed by children of all ages. Make the fruit syrup and freeze it for an hour or two so it is ready to blend to a slushy consistency. If you forget about it and the syrup freezes solid, let it thaw a little at room temperature or simply heat it for a few seconds in a microwave.

Makes 2–3 glasses

2 oranges
250g/9oz/2¼ cups blueberries
50g/2oz/4 tbsp caster (superfine) sugar

1 Using a small, sharp knife, carefully cut away the majority of the skin from the oranges, then cut the oranges into 8–10 chunky wedges of roughly the same size.

2 Reserve a few blueberries for decoration, then push the rest through a juicer, alternating them with the orange wedges.

3 Add the sugar and 300ml/½ pint/ 1¼ cups cold water to the juice and stir until the sugar has dissolved. Pour into a shallow, non-metallic freezer container and freeze for 1–2 hours or until the juice is beginning to freeze all over.

4 Use a fork to break up any solid areas of the mixture and tip into a blender or food processor. Blend until smooth and slushy. Spoon the drink into glasses and serve, topped with blueberries or other fruit.

Rainbow juice

Brightly coloured layers of pure fruit juice give this smoothie extra child-appeal. Strawberry, kiwi fruit and pineapple provide plenty of colour contrast but you can use almost any other fruits that blend to a fairly thick consistency, and create your own rainbow. Check the sweetness of each juice before layering up the fruits, stirring in a little sugar if necessary.

Makes 3 glasses

4 kiwi fruit
½ small pineapple
130g/4½oz/generous 1 cup strawberries

1 Using a sharp knife, peel the kiwi fruit. Cut away the skin from the pineapple, then halve and remove the core. Roughly chop the pineapple flesh.

2 Put the pineapple in a blender or food processor and add 30ml/2 tbsp water. Process to a smooth purée, scraping the mixture down from the side of the bowl with a rubber spatula, if necessary. Tip into a small bowl.

3 Add the kiwi fruit to the blender and blend until smooth. Tip into a separate bowl. Finally, blend the strawberries until smooth.

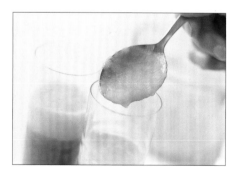

4 Pour the strawberry purée into three glass tumblers. Carefully spoon the kiwi fruit purée into the glasses to form a separate layer. Spoon the pineapple purée over the kiwi fruit and serve with spoons or thick straws.

Raspberry, banana and peach smoothie

Children will love this naturally sweet fruit drink. Whizzed up in just minutes, this thick, slightly tart smoothie makes a good stop-gap between meals, a brilliant, easy-to-eat breakfast or serves as a healthy – and very tasty – dessert.

1 Halve, stone (pit) and roughly chop the peach, break the banana into pieces and put both fruits in a blender or food processor. Blend until smooth, scraping the mixture down the side of the bowl if necessary.

2 Add the raspberries and blend until smooth. Pour into glasses and top up with mineral water, if using. Add ice cubes, decorate with extra raspberries and serve with straws or spoons.

Makes 2 small glasses

1 large ripe peach
1 small banana
130g/4½oz/¾ cup fresh or frozen
 raspberries, plus extra to decorate
still or sparkling mineral water (optional)
ice cubes

Cook's tip

If your children are fussy about the pips (seeds) in raspberries, blend them first and push the mixture through a fine sieve to remove the seeds, then return the purée to the blended banana mixture.

Top pops

Chunky ice-lolly stirrers give this fruit-packed smoothie plenty of child-appeal. It's great for a party or as an after-school treat on a hot day. The lollies can be frozen ahead and stored so they're ready on demand, and the juice takes just moments to prepare.

Makes 2 glasses

1 apple
300ml/½ pint/1¼ cups apple juice
2 kiwi fruit
90g/3½oz/generous ½ cup raspberries
10ml/2 tsp caster (superfine) sugar
150g/5oz/1 cup red grapes
150g/5oz/1¼ cups blackcurrants or
  blackberries
1 large banana

1 Peel, core and roughly chop the apple. Place in a food processor or blender with 100ml/3½fl oz/ scant ½ cup of the apple juice and blend to a smooth purée. Pour into a third of the sections of an ice-cube tray.

2 Peel and roughly chop the kiwi fruit and blend until smooth with 100ml of the apple juice. Pour into another third of the ice-cube tray sections.

3 Blend the raspberries with the sugar and the remaining apple juice and spoon into the final sections. Freeze the tray for about 30 minutes then push a wooden ice-lolly (popsicle) stick into each. Freeze until solid.

4 Put the grapes, blackcurrants or blackberries, and banana into the blender or food processor and blend until smooth. If you like, push the mixture through a coarse sieve after blending to remove the seeds and skins.

5 Push several of the fruit lollies out of the tray and place on separate plates for each child. Pour the fruit juice into two glasses and place on plates with the lollies. Serve immediately as the lollies will start to melt very quickly – and don't forget to supply the children with plenty of napkins.

Tropical fruit shake

Sweet, fruity and packed with vitamin C, this is a brilliant way to get children to enjoy healthy drinks. If you use really ripe fruit, it shouldn't need any additional sweetening, but taste it to check before serving. Mango makes a thick purée when blended, so top it up with mineral water – or try a good quality lemonade instead.

Makes 2 glasses

½ small pineapple
small bunch seedless white grapes
1 mango
mineral water or lemonade (optional)

1 Using a sharp knife, cut away the skin from the pineapple and halve the fruit. Discard the core and roughly chop the flesh of one half. Add to a blender or food processor with the grapes. Halve the mango either side of the flat stone (pit). Scoop the flesh into the blender.

2 Process thoroughly until really smooth, scraping the mixture down from the side of the bowl, if necessary. Pour into glasses and top up with mineral water or lemonade, if using. Serve immediately.

Cook's tip

For really fussy children, you might want to strain the mixture first. To do this, push it through a fine sieve, pressing the pulp in the sieve with the back of a spoon to extract as much juice as possible. Follow the recipe as normal, topping up the glasses with mineral water or lemonade if your children prefer it. To make a novelty decoration, thread pieces of fruit on to straws before you serve the shake.

Raspberry rippler

Colourful ripples of raspberry and mango give instant child appeal to this fruit-packed smoothie. Soya milk is so delicious and such a healthy alternative to cow's milk in drinks that it's worth trying, even for children who are not on a dairy-free diet. Here it's blended with mango to create a smooth, thick contrast to the tangy raspberries. For best results, use only really ripe, sweet mango.

Makes 2 glasses

90g/3½oz/generous ½ cup fresh or frozen raspberries, plus a few extra to decorate
15–30ml/1–2 tbsp clear honey
1 mango
100ml/3½fl oz/scant ½ cup soya milk

1 Process the raspberries in a blender or food processor until smooth. Add 15ml/1 tbsp water and 5–10ml/1–2 tsp of the honey to sweeten. Transfer to a small bowl and rinse out the blender or food processor bowl.

2 Halve the mango either side of the flat stone (pit). Scoop the flesh from the two halves and around the stone into the clean blender or food processor and process until smooth. Add the soya milk and 10–20ml/2–4 tsp honey to sweeten.

Cook's tip
It will make such a difference to your children's health, and to their general appreciation of food, if they can enjoy fresh, naturally sweet drinks like this. Try serving this smoothie as a refreshing dessert after a barbecue or a family meal – it makes a delicious alternative to the similarly named, but slightly less healthy, raspberry ripple ice cream.

3 Pour a 2.5cm/1in layer of the mango purée into two tumblers. Spoon half the raspberry purée on top. Add the remaining mango purée, then finish with the remaining raspberry purée. Using a teaspoon, lightly swirl the two mixtures together. Serve decorated with extra raspberries.

Candystripe

This wickedly indulgent drink combines freshly blended strawberries with a marshmallow flavoured cream, making a milkshake that adults as well as kids will find totally irresistible. There's no point even trying to resist the melting marshmallow sweetness of this cheeky little strawberry confection – just sit back and give yourself up.

Makes 4 large glasses

150g/5oz white and pink marshmallows
500ml/17fl oz/generous 2 cups full cream (whole) milk
60ml/4 tbsp redcurrant jelly
450g/1lb/4 cups strawberries
60ml/4 tbsp double (heavy) cream
extra strawberries and marshmallows, to decorate

1 Put the marshmallows in a heavy pan with half the milk and heat gently, stirring frequently until the marshmallows have melted. Leave to stand until it has cooled.

2 Heat the redcurrant jelly in a small pan until melted. Put the strawberries in a blender or food processor and process until smooth, scraping down the side of the bowl with a rubber spatula as often as is necessary.

3 Stir 10ml/2 tsp of the strawberry purée into the melted jelly. Set aside the strawberry syrup. Pour the remaining purée into a jug (pitcher) and add the marshmallow mixture, the cream and the remaining milk. Chill the milkshake and four large glasses for about 1 hour.

4 To serve, use a teaspoon to drizzle lines of the strawberry syrup down the insides of the glasses – this creates a candystripe effect when filled. Fill the glasses with the milkshake. Serve topped with the extra marshmallows and strawberries and drizzle with any leftover strawberry syrup.

Cook's tip
If you can convince the children to wait long enough, this blend will really benefit from being chilled in the refrigerator for a couple of hours before serving.

Peppermint crush

The next time you see seaside rock or the peppermint candy canes that are around at Christmas time, buy a few sticks for this incredibly easy, fun drink for children. All you need to do is whizz it up with some milk and freeze until slushy, so it's ready and waiting for thirsty youngsters. This shake could almost pass as a dessert, so try serving it after a meal.

Makes 4 glasses

90g/3½oz pink peppermint rock (rock candy)
750ml/1¼ pints/3 cups full cream (whole) or
   semi-skimmed (low-fat) milk
a few drops of pink food colouring (optional)
pink candy canes, to serve

Cook's tip
If you cannot find pink candy canes to use as novelty stirrers for this drink, buy peppermint lolly pops instead.

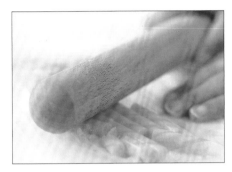

1 While the rock is still in its wrapper, hit with a rolling pin to break into small bits. (If unwrapped, put the rock in a polythene bag to crush it.) Tip the pieces into a blender or food processor.

2 Add the milk and a few drops of pink food colouring, if using, to the crushed rock and process until the rock is broken up into tiny pieces.

3 Pour the mixture into a shallow freezer container and freeze for about 2 hours or until turning slushy around the edges. Beat the mixture with a fork, breaking up the semi-frozen areas and stirring them into the centre.

4 Re-freeze and repeat the process once or twice more until the mixture is slushy. Spoon into glasses and serve with candy cane stirrers.

Custard cream float

This fabulously frothy dessert drink makes a wonderful treat that rounds off any meal brilliantly, or you could serve it to your children as a special snack mid-morning or at teatime.

Makes 3 glasses

75g/3oz custard cream biscuits (cookies)
1 large banana
5ml/1 tsp vanilla essence (extract)
200ml/7fl oz/scant 1 cup full cream
    (whole) milk
6 scoops vanilla ice cream
banana slices and crumbled biscuit
    (cookie), to decorate
drinking chocolate or cocoa powder
    (unsweetened), for dusting

Cook's tip
For an extra burst of banana flavour, use banana ice cream.

1 Put the custard cream biscuits in a blender or food processor and blend well until finely ground. Break the banana into chunks and add to the ground biscuits. Process thoroughly until a smooth, thick paste forms, scraping down the side of the bowl with a rubber spatula, if necessary.

2 Add the vanilla essence, milk and three scoops of the ice cream and process again until smooth and foamy. Pour into tumblers and top with the remaining scoops of ice cream. Decorate with banana slices and crumbled biscuit and serve dusted with a little drinking chocolate or cocoa powder.

Chocolate nut swirl

Children everywhere will be captivated by this fabulous chocolatey concoction. It is a mixture of melted milk chocolate, chocolate nut spread and creamy milk, marbled together to make an attractive and delicious drink. Adults who like chocolate will love it too.

Makes 2 tall glasses

40g/1½oz/3 tbsp chocolate hazelnut spread
400ml/14fl oz/1⅔ cups full cream
    (whole) milk
90g/3½oz milk chocolate
30ml/2 tbsp extra thick double (heavy)
    cream (optional)
a little crushed ice
2 chocolate flake bars, to serve

Cook's tip
This drink is extremely rich and filling and should probably be reserved for special occasions, but if you feel that using chocolate flakes as novelty stirrers is a bit too much chocolate for your children, serve the drink with multi-coloured straws or plastic stirrers instead.

1 Put the chocolate spread in a small bowl with 10ml/2 tsp of the milk. Stir well until smooth and glossy.

2 Chop the chocolate. Put 100ml/3½fl oz/scant ½ cup of the remaining milk in a small pan and add the chocolate pieces. Heat gently, stirring until the chocolate has dissolved. Remove from the heat and pour into a jug (pitcher). Leave to cool for 10 minutes, then stir in the remaining milk.

3 Using a teaspoon, dot the chocolate hazelnut mixture around the sides of two tall glasses, rotating them so that each glass is randomly streaked with chocolate. Dot the cream around the glasses in the same way, if using.

4 Put a little crushed ice in each glass and pour over the chocolate milk. Serve immediately with flake bar stirrers that can be used to swirl the hazelnut mixture into the chocolate milk.

crushes
and
slushes

What could be better than relaxing in the garden
on a hot afternoon enjoying an ice-cool, refreshing
blend? This chapter offers a fabulous fusion
of flavours, whether you prefer fat-free, refreshing
slushes such as cranberry, cinnamon and
ginger, or luxurious, creamy blends with white
chocolate, ice cream and hazelnuts.

Cool as a currant

Tiny, glossy blackcurrants are a virtual powerhouse of nutrients, packed with vitamins C and E, as well as essential iron, calcium and magnesium. Whizzed in a blender with plenty of crushed ice, they make a drink so deliciously thick and slushy that you might want to serve it with long spoons so that you can scoop up every last drop.

Makes 2 tall glasses

125g/4¼oz/generous 1 cup blackcurrants, plus extra to decorate
60ml/4 tbsp light muscovado (brown) sugar
good pinch of mixed (apple pie) spice (optional)
225g/8oz/2 cups crushed ice

1 Put the blackcurrants and sugar in a pan. (There is no need to string the blackcurrants first.) Add the mixed spice, if using, and pour in 100ml/3½fl oz/scant ½ cup water. Bring to the boil and cook for 2–3 minutes until the blackcurrants are completely soft.

2 Press the mixture through a sieve into a bowl, pressing the pulp with the back of a wooden spoon to extract as much juice as possible. Leave to stand until it has completely cooled.

Cook's tip
This is a great juice to make if you have plenty of blackcurrants in the freezer – they will thaw quickly in the pan. Redcurrants, or a mixture of redcurrants and blackcurrants, could also be used.

Make a double quantity of this juice and store it in the refrigerator for up to a week – then it can be quickly blended with ice whenever you like.

3 Put the crushed ice in a blender or food processor with the cooled juice and blend for about 1 minute until slushy. Pour into glasses, decorate with blackcurrants and serve immediately.

Cranberry, cinnamon and ginger spritzer

Partially freezing fruit juice gives it a wonderfully slushy texture that is very refreshing. The combination of cranberry and apple juice contributes a tart, clean flavour that's not too sweet.

Makes 4 glasses

600ml/1 pint/2½ cups chilled cranberry juice
150ml/¼ pint/⅔ cup clear apple juice
4 cinnamon sticks
about 400ml/14fl oz/1⅔ cups chilled
   ginger ale
a few fresh or frozen cranberries, to decorate

1 Pour the cranberry juice into a shallow freezer container and freeze for 2 hours or until a thick layer of ice crystals forms around the edges.

2 Mash with a fork to break up the ice, then return the mixture to the freezer for a further 2–3 hours until almost solid.

3 Pour the apple juice into a small saucepan, add two cinnamon sticks and bring to just below boiling point. Pour into a jug (pitcher) and leave to cool, then remove the cinnamon sticks and set aside with the others. Chill the juice until it is very cold.

4 Spoon the cranberry ice into a blender or food processor. Add the apple juice and blend until slushy. Pile into cocktail glasses, top up with ginger ale and decorate with the fresh or frozen cranberries. Pop a long cinnamon stick into each glass to use as a swizzle stick.

Cook's tip
As an alternative decoration, thread cranberries on to cocktail sticks (toothpicks) and add one to each glass instead of a cinnamon stick.

Strawberries and cream

Real strawberries and cream are really only worth eating when fresh strawberries are at their best, and the same goes for this delectable drink. Use small, vibrantly red and thoroughly ripe fruit. Frozen whole, they serve as flavour-packed ice cubes that will chill the drink.

Makes 2 tall glasses

275g/10oz/2½ cups small strawberries
15ml/1 tbsp lemon juice
5ml/1 tsp vanilla sugar
cream soda

Cook's tip
If you cannot find vanilla sugar in the supermarket, make your own. Fill a jar with caster (superfine) sugar and press a whole vanilla pod (bean) into the centre. Seal and leave for 2–3 weeks. As the sugar is used, simply top up the jar with more.

1 Hull the strawberries. Freeze about 130g/4½oz/generous 1 cup of the smallest strawberries for about 1 hour, or until firm. Process the remainder in a blender or food processor with the lemon juice and sugar until smooth, scraping the mixture down from the side of the bowl, if necessary.

2 Divide the frozen strawberries between two tall glasses and pour in the strawberry purée. Top up with cream soda and serve immediately with long-handled spoons so your guests can scoop out the delicious frozen strawberries and eat them – once they have defrosted slightly.

Apple refresher

Made using freshly juiced apples, this vibrant blend has a wonderfully crisp, thirst-quenching flavour. The really sweet, ripe fruits are juiced and then frozen until slushy. Served with additional apples and topped up with sparkling water, this drink couldn't be simpler.

Makes 3 glasses

6 large red eating apples
10ml/2 tsp lemon juice
a little clear honey (optional)
sparkling mineral water

Cook's tip
Green and red apples produce quite different flavours in juices. Red apples are better for this recipe because the colour is pretty and the flavour light and fragrant. Crisp, green apples will give a sweeter, tangier and denser flavour.

1 Reserve one of the apples. Quarter and core the remainder and cut the flesh into small pieces. Juice the apple pieces and stir in the lemon juice.

2 Check for sweetness, adding a little honey, if using. (Remember that the flavour will be less sweet once frozen.) Pour into a shallow freezer container, cover and freeze until a band of slush has formed around the edges.

3 Using a fork, break up the frozen apple juice, pushing it into the centre of the container. Re-freeze for 1 hour or until slushy all over. Again, break up the mixture with a fork.

4 Quarter and core the remaining apple and cut into thin slices. Spoon the slush into three glasses until two-thirds full and tuck the apple slices down the sides. Top up with sparkling water to serve.

Frosty fruits

Long after summer is over you can still summon up the glorious flavours of the season by making this fruity and refreshing drink from frozen summer fruits. This purple, slushy, fruity delight will pep up even the darkest mornings. Revitalize yourself with this blend before you leave for work in the morning to give your body a well-deserved boost.

1 Take the frozen fruits straight from the freezer and tip them into a blender or food processor. Blend until finely crushed, scraping down the side of the bowl, if necessary.

2 Add the yogurt and cream to the crushed fruit, then spoon in 30ml/ 2 tbsp of the sugar. Blend again until the mixture is smooth and thick. Taste and add the extra sugar if necessary. Serve immediately, decorated with fruit.

Makes 2–3 glasses

250g/9oz/2 cups frozen summer fruits, plus extra to decorate
200g/7oz/scant 1 cup natural (plain) yogurt
45ml/3 tbsp double (heavy) cream
30–45ml/2–3 tbsp caster (superfine) sugar

Cook's tip
This drink takes only moments to whizz up and you can use any mixture of fruits, whether you've grown your own berries or bought them frozen in bags.

Iced mango lassi

Based on a traditional Indian drink, this is perfect for any occasion: served with spicy food at dinner, at long, hot garden parties, or as a welcome cooler at any time of day. The yogurt ice that forms the basis of this drink is a useful recipe to add to your repertoire because it is much lighter and healthier than classic ice creams.

Makes 3–4 glasses

175g/6oz/scant 1 cup caster (superfine) sugar
150ml/¼ pint/⅔ cup water
2 lemons
500ml/17fl oz/generous 2 cups Greek
   (US strained plain) yogurt
350ml/12fl oz/1½ cups mango juice
ice cubes (optional)
fresh mint sprigs and mango wedges,
   to decorate

1 To make the yogurt ice, put the sugar and water in a saucepan and heat gently, stirring occasionally, until the sugar has dissolved. Pour the syrup into a jug (pitcher). Leave to cool, then chill until very cold.

2 Grate the rind from the lemons and then squeeze out the juice. Add the rind and juice to the chilled syrup and stir well to mix.

3 Pour the syrup mixture into a shallow, freezer container and freeze until thickened. Beat in the yogurt and return to the freezer until the mixture is thick enough to scoop.

4 To serve the drinks, briefly process the mango juice with about ten small scoops of yogurt ice in a blender or food processor until just smooth. Pour equal portions of the mixture into tall glasses or tumblers and add the ice cubes, if using.

5 Top each drink with another scoop of the yogurt ice and decorate with mint sprigs and mango wedges. Serve.

Fire and ice

Tickle your tastebuds with this unconventional frozen yogurt drink that is flavoured with fresh orange juice and specks of hot red chilli. It's great on a hot summer's day, after lunch or any other time when you're in need of a refreshing boost. If you've plenty of time on your hands, add an alcoholic kick to the drink by drizzling each glass with a splash of orange liqueur before serving.

Makes 2–3 tall glasses

90g/3½oz/½ cup caster (superfine) sugar
1 lemon
300ml/½ pint/1¼ cups freshly squeezed
    orange juice
200g/7oz/scant 1 cup Greek (US strained
    plain) yogurt
1 red chilli, seeded and finely chopped
60ml/4 tbsp Cointreau or other orange-
    flavoured liqueur (optional)
orange slices and extra chillies, to decorate

1 Put the sugar in a pan with 100ml/ 3½fl oz/scant ½ cup water and heat gently, stirring with a spoon until the sugar has dissolved. Pour into a freezer container and leave to cool. Finely grate the rind of the lemon and juice.

2 Add the lemon rind and juice and 100ml/3½fl oz/scant ½ cup of the orange juice. Freeze for 2 hours or until a band of ice has formed around the edges. Turn into a bowl and add the yogurt and chopped chilli. Whisk until thick. Freeze for 1–2 hours until almost solid.

3 To serve, scoop the frozen yogurt into a blender or food processor and add the remaining orange juice. Process until very thick and smooth. Pour into tall glasses and drizzle with a little liqueur, if using. Serve with straws and decorate with orange slices and fresh chillies.

Cook's tip
Don't worry if you forget to remove the chilli yogurt from the freezer before it has frozen solid. Leave it at room temperature for a while to soften or simply heat it briefly in a microwave.

Pineapple and yogurt ice

Cooling and delicious yogurt ice can be bought in several flavours, including vanilla, orange and lemon, and is perfect in summer drinks as a lighter alternative to traditional ice cream. Use a really sweet, juicy pineapple and fresh, pungent basil to add plenty of vibrant colour and exotic flavour to this refreshing iced drink.

1 Remove the basil leaves from the stems and tear them into small pieces. Cut away the skin from the pineapple, then halve the fruit and remove the core. Chop the flesh into chunks. Push the pineapple through a juicer with the basil. Chill until ready to serve.

2 Pour the juice into tall glasses and add two scoops of yogurt ice to each. Decorate with basil sprigs and dust lightly with icing sugar.

Makes 2 glasses

25g/1oz fresh basil, plus extra sprigs
   to decorate
1 pineapple
4 large scoops vanilla-, lemon- or
   orange-flavoured yogurt ice
icing (confectioners') sugar, for dusting

Cook's tip
Fresh mint makes an equally refreshing alternative to basil if you have plenty growing in the garden, or try other soft-leaved herbs, such as lemon balm.

White chocolate and hazelnut cream

This luxurious combination of smooth, creamy white chocolate and crunchy hazelnut is simply irresistible. To get the maximum flavour from the hazelnuts, it is always best to use whole ones, toasting them first to develop their nuttiness and then grinding them fresh, rather than using ready chopped or ground nuts.

Makes 3 glasses

90g/3½oz/scant 1 cup blanched hazelnuts
150g/5oz white chocolate
300ml/½ pint/1¼ cups full cream
    (whole) milk
4 large scoops white chocolate or vanilla
    ice cream
a little freshly grated nutmeg (optional)

1 Roughly chop the hazelnuts using a large, sharp knife, then toast them lightly in a dry frying pan, turning continuously to ensure that they are toasted evenly. Reserve 30ml/2 tbsp for decoration, then tip the remainder into a blender or food processor. Blend until very finely ground.

2 Finely chop the chocolate and reserve 30ml/2 tbsp for decoration. Put the remainder in a small, heavy pan with half of the milk and heat very gently until the chocolate has melted thoroughly. Stir until smooth, then pour the chocolate into a bowl. Add the remaining milk, stir and leave to cool.

3 Add the melted chocolate mixture to the blender with the ice cream and a little grated nutmeg, if using. Blend until the mixture is smooth. Pour into glasses and sprinkle with the reserved hazelnuts and chocolate. Grate over a little extra nutmeg, if you like, and serve immediately.

Ice cool coconut

This fabulously cooling, dairy-free drink is just about as silky smooth as they come. Rather than using coconut milk, this recipe opts for desiccated coconut, steeped in water, which is then strained to extract the flavour. Without the nutty texture, this delicious coconut feast slides down very nicely on a summer's evening. If it's the weekend – or even if it's not – and you fancy a bit of a treat, add a splash of Malibu or coconut-flavoured liqueur.

Makes 2–3 glasses

150g/5oz/2½ cups desiccated (dry
    unsweetened shredded) coconut
30ml/2 tbsp lime juice
30ml/2 tbsp icing (confectioners') sugar, plus
    extra for dusting
200g/7oz vanilla iced non-dairy dessert
lime slices, to decorate

Cook's tip
Desiccated coconut can be bought ready sweetened. If using this, you may wish to omit the sugar that's added with the lime juice.

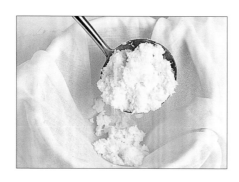

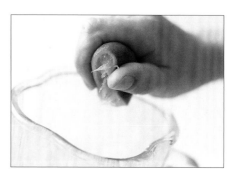

1 Put the coconut in a heatproof bowl and add 600ml/1 pint/2½ cups boiling water. Leave to stand for 30 minutes. Strain the coconut through a sieve lined with muslin (cheesecloth) into a bowl, pressing the pulp with a spoon to extract as much juice as possible. Discard the pulp and chill the coconut milk.

2 Pour the coconut milk into a blender or food processor with the lime juice, sugar and non-dairy dessert. Blend thoroughly until completely smooth. Pour into glasses and decorate with lime slices. Lightly dust the lime slices and edges of the glasses with icing sugar and serve immediately.

Rum and raisin thick-shake

This rich and creamy milkshake, based on the classic combination of rum and raisins, is remarkably easy to prepare. Use a good quality ice cream, leave it to soften slightly in the refrigerator before scooping, and you simply can't go wrong. If the raisins are a little dry, leave them to soak in the rum for a few minutes to soften and plump up before you blend them.

1 Put the raisins, rum and a little of the milk into a blender or food processor and process for about 1 minute, or until the raisins are finely chopped.

2 Spoon two large scoops of the vanilla ice cream into two tall glasses and put the remaining ice cream and milk into the blender. Process until creamy.

3 Pour the milkshake into glasses and serve immediately with straws and long spoons for scooping up the raisins.

Makes 2 tall glasses

75g/3oz/generous ½ cup raisins
45ml/3 tbsp dark rum
300ml/½ pint/1¼ cups full cream (whole) milk
500ml/17fl oz/2¼ cups good quality vanilla ice cream

Cook's tip
As an alternative, replace the vanilla ice cream with a good quality chocolate-flavoured ice cream – this will taste exceptionally good with rum and raisins.

Espresso crush

A fresh update on iced coffee, this creatively layered treat combines slushy frozen granita with a thick vanilla ice cream layer, and is perfect for rounding off a lazy summer lunch or as a late afternoon refresher. The granita needs several hours in the freezer but will then keep for weeks so it is ready and waiting whenever you fancy a burst of ice-cold espresso.

Makes 4 glasses

75ml/5 tbsp ground espresso coffee
75g/3oz/scant ½ cup caster (superfine) sugar
300g/11oz vanilla ice cream or
   vanilla iced non-dairy dessert
75ml/5 tbsp milk or soya milk

1 Put the coffee in a cafetière (press pot), add 750ml/1¼ pints/3 cups boiling water and leave to infuse for 5 minutes. Plunge the cafetière and pour the coffee into a shallow freezer container. Stir in the sugar until dissolved. Leave to cool completely, then cover and freeze for about 2 hours or until the mixture starts to turn slushy around the edges.

2 Using a fork, break up the ice crystals, stirring them into the centre of the container. Re-freeze until the mixture is slushy around the edges again. Repeat forking and stirring once or twice more until the mixture is completely slushy and there is no liquid remaining. Re-freeze until ready to use.

Cook's tip
The softened ice cream will melt quickly once you start layering it up in the glasses, so a good trick is to thoroughly chill the glasses before using them.

3 Put the ice cream or iced dessert and milk in a blender or food processor and process until thick and smooth. To serve, spoon a little into the base of each glass and sprinkle with a layer of the granita. Repeat layering until the glasses are full. Serve immediately.

tempting
dessert
drinks

Irresistible blends that imitate popular desserts are
cleverly transformed into stunning drinks you can
sip leisurely or, in some cases, scoop with a spoon.
Be tempted by true classics such as raspberry
brûlée cream and blueberry meringue or, for
something a bit different, try a spicy rhubarb milk
and an unusual take on traditional banoffee pie.

Sparkling peach melba

Serve this delightfully fresh and fruity drink during the summer months when raspberries and peaches are at their sweetest and best. Traditional cream soda gives this drink a really smooth flavour and a lovely fizz, while the optional shot of Drambuie or brandy gives it a definite kick. Serve with long spoons for scooping up any fruit left in the glasses.

Makes 2 glasses

300g/11oz/scant 2 cups raspberries
2 large ripe peaches
30ml/2 tbsp Drambuie or brandy (optional)
15ml/1 tbsp icing (confectioners') sugar
cream soda, to serve

1 Pack a few raspberries into six tiny shot glasses, or into six sections of an ice cube tray, and pour over water to cover. Freeze for several hours.

2 Using a small, sharp knife, halve and stone (pit) the peaches and cut one half into thin slices. Reserve 115g/4oz/ ⅔ cup of the raspberries and divide the rest, along with the peach slices, between two tall stemmed glasses. Drizzle with the liqueur, if using.

3 Push the reserved raspberries and the remaining peach flesh through the juicer. Stir the icing sugar into the juice and pour the juice over the fruits.

Cook's tip
If using shot glasses, dip these into a bowl of warm water for a few seconds to loosen the blocks of frozen raspberries. If using ice cube trays, turn these upside down and hold under warm running water for a few seconds. The ice cubes should then pop out easily.

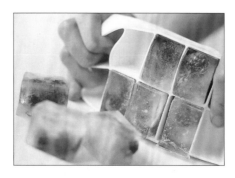

4 Turn the raspberry-filled ice cubes out of the shot glasses or ice cube tray and add three to each glass. Top up with cream soda and serve immediately.

Super sorbet fizz

Freshly blended pineapple and cool, tangy lemon sorbet, topped up with sparkling ginger ale, makes a tastebud-tingling, fantastically mouthwatering drink. This semi-frozen blend is perfect after a summer lunch as a light alternative to more conventional desserts, or as a drink that can be whizzed up to allow you to chill out whenever the mood takes you.

Makes 4 glasses

30ml/2 tbsp muscovado (molasses) sugar
15ml/1 tbsp lemon juice
½ pineapple
1 piece preserved stem ginger,
   roughly chopped
200ml/7fl oz/scant 1 cup lemon sorbet,
   slightly softened
wafer thin pineapple and lemon slices,
   to decorate
ginger ale, to serve

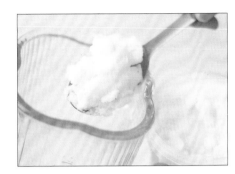

3 Add the sorbet and process briefly until smooth. Spoon the muscovado syrup into four tumblers, then pour in the pineapple mixture.

4 Decorate the edge of the glasses with the pineapple and lemon slices. Top up each glass with ginger ale and serve immediately.

Cook's tip
The easiest way to prepare a pineapple is to chop off the top and base, then slice off the skin. Use the tip of a sharp knife to remove the "eyes" and then roughly chop into chunks.

1 Mix the sugar with the lemon juice in a small bowl and leave to stand for about 5 minutes until it turns syrupy.

2 Discard the skin and core from the pineapple and cut the flesh into chunks. Put the chunks in a blender or food processor with the ginger and whizz until smooth, scraping down the side of the bowl once or twice, if necessary.

Black beauty

This refreshing drink celebrates the perfect, classic partnership of apples and tart blackberries. The sweetness of the apples is balanced deliciously by the sharp tang and vibrant colour of the ripe berries. If you cannot find fresh blackberries, other deep red fruits such as mulberries or loganberries can be used as an equally irresistible substitute.

Makes 2–3 tall glasses

30ml/2 tbsp golden sugar
2.5ml/½ tsp ground cinnamon
3 eating apples
200g/7oz/1¾ cups blackberries
ice cubes
borage, to decorate (optional)

Cook's tip
This drink will taste best if you've picked the blackberries yourself. If you can't find them, however, other fruits will work just as well, or you could use frozen blackberries.

1 Put the golden sugar in a small bowl. Add the cinnamon and 60ml/4 tbsp boiling water and stir until the sugar dissolves to form a syrup.

2 Roughly chop the apples. Push the blackberries through a juicer and follow with the apples. Pour in the sugar syrup and stir well to mix.

3 Pour the juice into tall glasses and add several ice cubes to each one. Decorate the drinks with sprigs of borage or individual borage flowers, if using, and serve immediately.

Blueberry meringue crumble

Imagine the most appealing flavours of a blueberry meringue dessert – fresh tangy fruit, crisp sugary meringue and plenty of vanilla-scented cream. This drink combines all of these in one delicious milkshake. Iced yogurt is used to provide a slightly lighter note than ice cream, but there's nothing to stop you using ice cream instead for an even greater indulgence.

1 Put the blueberries and sugar in a blender or food processor with 60ml/ 4 tbsp water and blend until smooth, scraping the mixture down from the side once or twice, if necessary.

2 Transfer the purée to a small bowl and rinse out the blender or food processor bowl to get rid of any remaining blueberry juice.

3 Put the iced yogurt, milk and lime juice in the blender and process until thoroughly combined. Add half of the crushed meringues and process again until smooth.

4 Carefully pour alternate layers of the milkshake, blueberry syrup and the remaining crushed meringues into tall glasses, finishing with a few chunky pieces of meringue.

5 Drizzle any remaining blueberry syrup over the tops of the meringues and decorate with a few extra blueberries. Serve immediately.

Makes 3–4 tall glasses

150g/5oz/1¼ cups fresh blueberries,
   plus extra to decorate
15ml/1 tbsp icing (confectioners') sugar
250ml/8fl oz/1 cup vanilla iced yogurt
200ml/7fl oz/scant 1 cup full cream
   (whole) milk
30ml/2 tbsp lime juice
75g/3oz meringues, lightly crushed

Cook's tip
The easiest way to crush the meringues is to put them in a plastic bag on a work surface and tap them gently with a rolling pin. Stop tapping the meringues as soon as they have crumbled into little bitesize pieces otherwise you'll just be left with tiny crumbs.

Raspberry brûlée cream

This recipe, based on a classic French dessert, takes a little more preparation than most drinks but is well worth the extra effort. Like all the best brûlée recipes it starts with a home-made custard, so you'll need to be patient and allow time for it to thicken and chill.

Makes 4 glasses

800ml/1⅓ pints/3½ cups full cream
   (whole) milk
3 large egg yolks
130g/4½oz/scant ¾ cup caster
   (superfine) sugar
5ml/1 tsp vanilla essence (extract)
15ml/1 tbsp cornflour (cornstarch)
250g/9oz/1½ cups fresh or frozen raspberries
extra raspberries and mint or lemon balm
   sprigs, to decorate

1 Pour 300ml/½ pint/1¼ cups of milk into sections of an ice-cube tray and freeze for 1 hour. Put the egg yolks in a bowl with 50g/2oz/¼ cup of the sugar, the vanilla essence and cornflour. Beat until smooth. Bring the remaining milk to the boil in a pan. Pour the milk over the yolk mixture, whisking until smooth.

2 Return the custard to the pan and cook over the lowest heat, stirring until slightly thickened. (The custard should start to thicken as the steam rises; take care not to overheat it or it may curdle.)

3 Pour the custard into a jug (pitcher), cover the surface with a round of greaseproof (waxed) paper to prevent a skin forming and leave to cool. Once cool, chill until ready to serve.

4 Line a baking sheet with baking parchment. Heat the remaining sugar in a pan with 60ml/4 tbsp water until the sugar has dissolved. Bring to the boil and boil for 3–5 minutes until the syrup turns a golden caramel colour. Plunge the base of the pan in cold water to prevent further cooking.

5 Using a dessertspoon, "scribble" the caramel on to the baking sheet to make four decorative circles. Leave to set.

6 Divide the raspberries among the glasses and mash lightly. In a blender or food processor, blend the custard with the milk ice cubes until lightly broken. Ladle the mixture over the fruit. Balance the caramel on top of the glasses and decorate with extra raspberries, mint or lemon balm sprigs.

Strawberry trifle

This wonderfully indulgent recipe takes the tastiest components of a classic trifle – the fruit, cream, nuts and a dash of liqueur – and combines them with ice cream to make a positive feast of a drink. Serve this blend as soon as it is assembled because the ingredients will swirl together in the glass fairly quickly and the pretty marbling effect will be lost.

Makes 4 glasses

2 eating apples
500g/1¼lb/5 cups strawberries
15ml/1 tbsp caster (superfine) sugar
60ml/4 tbsp sherry or Marsala
150ml/¼ pint/⅔ cup double (heavy)
   or whipping cream
60ml/4 tbsp flaked (sliced) almonds,
   lightly toasted
4 large scoops of vanilla ice cream

Cook's tip
As an alternative to vanilla ice cream use strawberry ice cream.

1 Quarter and core the apples then roughly chop the flesh. Hull and halve 200g/7oz/1¾ cups of the strawberries and set aside. Push the remaining strawberries and the apples through the juicer and stir in the sugar and sherry or Marsala. Chill until ready to serve.

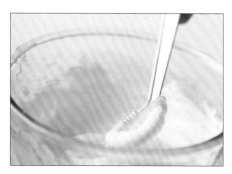

2 Lightly whip the cream until it is barely holding its shape. Put the strawberries into chilled glasses and sprinkle with half the nuts. Add a scoop of ice cream to each. Pour over the strawberry juice and top with the whipped cream. Decorate with the remaining nuts and serve.

Rhubarb and allspice cream

Pale shoots of young rhubarb, poached with sugar and spice, and blended with cream, make a truly dreamy concoction. Make this delicious blend early in the season otherwise the rhubarb stalks will be tougher, possibly stringy, and so acidic that you'll need heaps of sugar to make this the indulgent treat that it should be. Serve with a spoon to scoop up every last drop.

2 Transfer the rhubarb and cooking juice to a blender or food processor and process in short bursts until smooth, scraping down the mixture from the side of the bowl, if necessary.

3 Add the cream and milk to the rhubarb purée and blend again until combined. Transfer to a jug (pitcher) and chill until ready to serve.

4 Half-fill glasses with crushed ice, if using, pour over the juice, sprinkle with allspice and serve immediately.

Cook's tip

If you don't have fresh oranges to squeeze for this drink, you can use orange juice from a carton instead, or try a mix of citrus juices.

Makes 4 glasses

500g/1¼lb early rhubarb
100ml/3½fl oz/scant ½ cup freshly squeezed orange juice
75g/3oz/scant ½ cup caster (superfine) sugar
2.5ml/½ tsp ground allspice, plus extra to decorate
100ml/3½fl oz/scant ½ cup double (heavy) cream
200ml/7fl oz/scant 1 cup full cream (whole) milk
crushed ice (optional)

1 Trim the rhubarb and cut it into chunks. Put in a pan with the orange juice, sugar and allspice and bring to the boil. Cover and simmer gently for 6–8 minutes until tender. Remove the pan from the heat and leave to cool.

Turkish delight

If you like Turkish delight, you'll love this fabulously indulgent drink. With the scented aroma of rose water and the delicious icy sweetness of vanilla ice cream, it is difficult to imagine a more decadent, or delicious, combination of ingredients.

Makes 3–4 glasses

125g/4¼oz rose-flavoured Turkish delight
475ml/16fl oz/2 cups semi-skimmed (low-fat) milk
250ml/8fl oz/1 cup good quality vanilla ice cream
a little finely grated plain (semisweet) chocolate, or drinking chocolate powder, for sprinkling (optional)

Cook's tips
For an even frothier top on this drink, pour the milkshake into a large bowl and whisk with a hand-held electric mixer.

If the Turkish delight is very sticky, you'll find it easier to cut it with scissors instead of a knife.

1 Roughly chop the Turkish delight and reserve a few pieces for decoration. Put the rest in a pan with half the milk. Heat gently until the pieces begin to melt. Remove the pan from the heat and leave to cool.

2 Spoon the mixture into a blender or food processor and add the remaining milk. Process until smooth, then add the ice cream and blend briefly to combine. Pour into glasses, top with the reserved Turkish delight and serve, sprinkled with chocolate or drinking chocolate, if using.

Nutty nougat

For the best results, chill this glorious milkshake for a few hours until it is icy cold and the jumble of ingredients has had time to merge into a hedonistic fusion of flavours. Skinning the pistachio nuts is not essential, but it makes a fabulous visual impact, transforming the specks of nut from a dull green to a gorgeous, vivid emerald colour.

Makes 3 glasses

90ml/6 tbsp sweetened condensed milk
300ml/½ pint/1¼ cups semi-skimmed
  (low-fat) milk
100ml/3½fl oz/scant ½ cup crème fraîche
15ml/1 tbsp lemon juice
25g/1oz/¼ cup skinned pistachio nuts
25g/1oz/¼ cup blanched almonds
25g/1oz/3 tbsp candied peel, finely chopped,
  plus a few extra slices for decoration
ice cubes

2 Add the lemon juice, pistachio nuts, almonds and chopped peel to the blender or food processor and blend until chopped into tiny pieces. Pour over ice cubes in glasses, add a few slices of candied peel and serve.

Cook's tip

Pretty, emerald-green flecks of pistachio nut pepper this rich, nougat-flavoured milkshake, giving it the subtlest hint of colour and the most wonderful texture.

To skin the pistachio nuts, put them in a heatproof bowl, cover with boiling water and leave for about 2 minutes. Drain the nuts and rub them between layers of kitchen paper to loosen the skins. Pick out the nuts, carefully peeling off the remaining skin.

1 Put the condensed milk and the semi-skimmed milk in a blender or food processor. Add the crème fraîche and blend until combined.

Banoffee high

Make plenty of this outrageous, lip-smacking milkshake because everyone will love it. Nobody is pretending this is a health drink, but it is guaranteed to give you an energy rush of astronomic proportions. Keep any leftover syrup in the refrigerator to use as a quick and delicious toffee sauce for spooning over ice cream.

1 To make the toffee syrup, put the sugar in a small heavy pan with 75ml/ 5 tbsp water. Heat gently, stirring until the sugar dissolves, then add 45ml/ 3 tbsp of the cream and bring to the boil. Let the syrup simmer for about 4 minutes until thickened. Remove from the heat and leave to cool for about 30 minutes.

2 Peel the bananas, break into pieces and put into a blender or food processor with the milk, vanilla sugar, ice cubes and a further 45ml/3 tbsp of the cream. Blend until smooth and frothy.

3 Pour the remaining cream into a bowl and whip lightly with a whisk or hand-held electric mixer until it just holds its shape.

4 Add half the toffee syrup to the milkshake and blend, then pour into glasses. Drizzle more syrup around the insides of the glasses. Spoon the whipped cream over and drizzle with any remaining syrup. Serve immediately.

Makes 4 tall glasses

75g/3oz/scant ½ cup light muscovado (brown) sugar
150ml/¼ pint/⅔ cup double (heavy) cream
4 large bananas
600ml/1 pint/2½ cups full cream (whole) milk
15ml/1 tbsp vanilla sugar
8 ice cubes

Cook's tips
If you use a blender, read the instructions to check whether it is powerful enough to cope with crushing ice cubes.

Make the syrup a little in advance so it has time to thicken.

Coconut and passion fruit ice

Few things beat the unadulterated, pure flavour of freshly juiced coconut. Whizzed with plenty of crushed ice and teamed with sharp, intensely flavoured passion fruit, it produces a milkshake that tastes indulgently good but is still refreshingly natural and wholesome.

Makes 2–3 tall glasses

1 coconut
75ml/5 tbsp icing (confectioners') sugar
3 passion fruit
150g/5oz crushed ice
60ml/4 tbsp double (heavy) cream

Cook's tip
This tropical, icy, passionately luxurious drink is heavenly on a summer's evening. You don't have to be on holiday to enjoy this type of decadence as this drink can be made quickly and easily at any time. Make a jug full and share with friends or family – if you feel that you are able to share it.

1 Drain the milk from the coconut and put to one side. Break open the coconut, remove the flesh, then pare off the brown skin. Push the coconut pieces through a juicer along with 150ml/¼ pint/⅔ cup water. Stir the icing sugar into the juice and reserve.

2 Halve the passion fruit and scoop the pulp into a small bowl. Set aside.

3 Put the crushed ice in a blender or food processor and blend until slushy. Add the juiced coconut, any drained coconut milk and the cream. Process to just blend the ingredients.

4 Pour the mixture into tall stemmed glasses, then, using a teaspoon, spoon the passion fruit on top of the drink. Add stirrers, if you like, and serve.

Death by chocolate

There are only two ingredients used in this decadently rich smoothie: creamy milk and the best chocolate you can buy. Blended together, they make the frothiest, smoothest and most deliciously chocolatey drink you will ever taste. Once you've tried this recipe, you will never view a chocolate smoothie in the same light again.

Makes 2 large glasses

150g/5oz good quality chocolate
350ml/12fl oz/1½ cups full cream (whole) milk
ice cubes
chocolate curls or shavings, to serve

Cook's tip
Depending on personal taste, use dark (bittersweet) chocolate with 70 per cent cocoa solids, or a good quality milk chocolate. If you like the intensity of dark chocolate but the creaminess of milk, try using half of each type.

1 Break the chocolate into pieces and place in a heatproof bowl set over a pan of simmering water, making sure that the bowl does not rest in the water.

2 Add 60ml/4 tbsp of the milk and leave until the chocolate melts, stirring occasionally with a wooden spoon.

3 Remove the bowl from the heat, pour the remaining milk over the chocolate and stir to combine.

4 Pour the mixture into a blender or food processor and blend until frothy. Pour into glasses, add ice and chocolate curls or shavings, then serve.

Coffee frappé

This creamy, smooth creation, which is strictly for adults (because of the alcoholic content), makes a wonderful alternative to a dessert on a hot summer's evening – or indeed at any time when you feel you need to indulge yourself. Serve in small glasses or little cappuccino cups for a glamorous touch, and provide your guests with both straws and long-handled spoons to allow them to scoop out every last bit of this delicious drink.

Makes 4 glasses

8 scoops of classic coffee ice cream
90ml/6 tbsp Kahlúa or Tia Maria liqueur
150ml/¼ pint/⅔ cup single (light) cream
1.5ml/¼ tsp ground cinnamon (optional)
crushed ice
ground cinnamon, for sprinkling

Cook's tip
To make a non-alcoholic version of this drink, simply substitute strong black coffee for the Kahlúa or Tia Maria.

1 Put half the coffee ice cream in a food processor or blender. Add the liqueur, then pour in the cream with a little cinnamon, if using, and blend. Scoop the remaining ice cream into four glasses or cappuccino cups.

2 Using a dessertspoon, spoon the coffee cream over the ice cream in each glass, then top with a little crushed ice. Sprinkle the top of each frappé with a little ground cinnamon and serve immediately.

Cool chocolate float

Frothy, chocolatey milkshake and scoops of creamy sweet chocolate and vanilla ice cream are combined here to make the most meltingly delicious drink ever, which is sure to prove a big success with children and adults alike. If you simply adore chocolate and you love ice cream, this may be the perfect drink for you. As this is such a rich, indulgent blend, however, try and resist temptation and don't indulge too often – save it for very special occasions.

Makes 2 tall glasses

115g/4oz plain (semisweet) chocolate, broken
    into pieces
250ml/8fl oz/1 cup milk
15ml/1 tbsp caster (superfine) sugar
4 large scoops of classic vanilla ice cream
4 large scoops of dark (bittersweet) chocolate
    ice cream
a little lightly whipped cream
grated chocolate or chocolate curls,
    to decorate

Cook's tip
Try substituting banana, coconut or toffee ice cream for the chocolate and vanilla ice cream if you prefer.

1 Put the chocolate in a heavy pan and add the milk and sugar. Heat gently, stirring with a wooden spoon until the chocolate has melted and the mixture is smooth. Leave to cool.

2 Blend the cooled chocolate mixture with half of the ice cream in a blender or food processor.

3 Scoop the remaining ice cream alternately into two tall glasses: vanilla then chocolate. Using a dessertspoon, drizzle the chocolate milk over and around the ice cream in each glass. Top with lightly whipped cream and sprinkle over a little grated chocolate or some chocolate curls to decorate. Serve immediately.

real
boozy
blends

If you're entertaining friends or simply relaxing after a hard day's work, try one of these tasty tipples, which are guaranteed to put everyone in a mellow mood. Some are fruity and only mildly alcoholic, while others are spirit-based and pack a real punch – there's something here to suit every occasion.

Iced strawberry daiquiri

The classic daiquiri cocktail is named after a village in Cuba that lies near the Bacardi processing plant. The original version was an incredibly potent blend of rum and whisky but the fruit versions, which are so popular today, are slightly less alcoholic. This one combines sweet and fragrant strawberries with white rum and refreshingly tangy lime juice.

Makes 4 small glasses

4 limes
60ml/4 tbsp icing (confectioners') sugar
200ml/7fl oz/scant 1 cup white rum
275g/10oz/2½ cups strawberries
300g/11oz crushed ice

Cook's tip
To make a really slushy, thick iced daiquiri, use frozen strawberries. There's no need to leave them to thaw, just use them as they are.

To make a banana version of this drink, replace the strawberries with two bananas. Peel the bananas, break them into pieces and add with the rum and icing sugar.

1 Squeeze the limes and pour the juice into a blender or food processor. Add the icing sugar, rum and all but two of the strawberries. Process until really smooth and frothy.

2 Add the crushed ice to the blender or food processor and blend until slushy. Pour the daiquiri into glasses, add a strawberry half to each glass and serve.

Frozen margarita

For the serious cocktail connoisseur, a margarita sipped with a slice of lime from the salt-crusted rim of a glass is simply the best choice. A classic citrus juicer will help you to get the maximum juice from limes, but if the fruits are very firm and don't yield much juice, you could try giving them a brief blast in the microwave first.

1 To coat the glass rims with salt, put 30ml/2 tbsp of the lime juice into a saucer and plenty of salt flakes in another. Turn the glasses upside down and dip the rim of each glass in the lime juice, then in the salt. Invert the glasses again and put to one side.

2 Put the remaining lime juice in a blender or food processor with the Cointreau or Grand Marnier, tequila and ice. Process until the mixture is slushy.

3 Pour the margarita mixture into the salt-rimmed glasses, add a slice of lime to each glass and serve immediately.

Makes 8 small glasses

150ml/¼ pint/⅔ cup lime juice, from about
   6 large limes
sea salt flakes
120ml/4fl oz/½ cup Cointreau or
   Grand Marnier
200ml/7fl oz/scant 1 cup tequila
150g/5oz crushed ice
1 lime, thinly sliced, to decorate

Cook's tip
Gold tequila has aged in casks for longer than white and has a slightly golden tinge to it. Try to use clear tequila for this recipe as it will result in a fresh, clear cocktail in which the colour of the lime really shows through.

Raspberry rendezvous

Pink, raspberry-flavoured bubbles and a suspicion of brandy make this the ultimate in sippable sophistication. A splash of sweet, sugary grenadine added to the jewel-coloured raspberry juice will smooth out any hint of a sharp tang that there might be from slightly underripe fruit.

Makes 6 tall glasses

400g/14oz/2⅓ cups raspberries, plus extra raspberries, to serve
100ml/3½ fl oz/scant ½ cup grenadine
100ml/3½ fl oz/scant ½ cup brandy or cherry brandy
ice cubes
1 litre/1¾ pints/4 cups ginger ale

Cook's tip
Grenadine is a sweet, ruby-coloured syrup made from pomegranates. It is popularly used to enhance fruit juices and cocktails. True grenadine contains no alcohol, but there are alcoholic versions around.

1 Push handfuls of the raspberries through a juicer and transfer the juice into a jug (pitcher).

2 Stir the grenadine and brandy or cherry brandy into the raspberry juice and chill (preferably overnight, but for at least 1 or 2 hours) until you are ready to serve it.

3 Prepare six tall glasses: add plenty of ice cubes to each and place a few extra raspberries in the bottom of the glasses.

4 Pour the raspberry mixture into each of the prepared glasses and then top up with the ginger ale. Serve the cocktails immediately.

Scent sensation

Orange flower water, which is distilled from the delicate white blooms of the orange blossom tree, gives delicious sweet pear and redcurrant juices a delicate fragrance and a subtle, barely there flavour. Like rose water, it is often associated with Middle Eastern cooking and goes really well with warm-flavoured spices such as cinnamon.

Makes 4–5 glasses

4 pears
300g/11oz/2¾ cups redcurrants
2 cinnamon sticks
45ml/3 tbsp orange flower water
about 25g/1oz/¼ cup icing (confectioners') sugar
tonic water
cinnamon sticks and extra redcurrants, to decorate (optional)

Cook's tip
If you like, add a splash of alcohol; try an almond liqueur, such as Disaronno, as the almondy edge goes well with the scented flavours.

1 Using a small, sharp knife, cut the pears into chunks of roughly the same size and push the chunks through a juicer with the redcurrants.

2 Crumble the 2 cinnamon sticks, using your fingers, and add to the redcurrant juice. Cover and leave to stand for at least 1 hour.

3 Strain the juice through a sieve into a bowl, then whisk in the orange flower water and a little icing sugar to taste.

4 To serve, put one or two cinnamon sticks in each glass, if using. Pour the juice into glasses, then top up with tonic water and decorate with the extra redcurrants, if you like.

Watermelon gin

The fabulously red, juicy flesh of the watermelon makes a perfect partner for the strong, heady scent and flavour of gin. The juice is so sweet and delicate, and this sparkling drink is so stunningly pretty, that you'll be hard-pressed to resist its appeal. For a party, just make up a large jug of the juice, top up with tonic water and pour out for guests as they arrive.

1 Cut off the skin from the watermelon and chop the flesh into large chunks, removing the seeds. Push the flesh through the juicer and pour into a large jug (pitcher). Stir in the lime juice and sugar and chill.

2 Half-fill glasses with crushed ice. Stir the gin into the juice and pour over the ice. Add the lime slices and top up with tonic water. Serve immediately.

Makes 4 large glasses

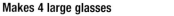

500g/1¼lb wedge watermelon
juice of 1 lime
10ml/2 tsp caster (superfine) sugar
crushed ice
150ml/¼ pint/⅔ cup gin
lime slices
tonic water

Cook's tip
This recipe makes a cocktail that is not too alcoholic. If you would prefer a slightly stronger drink, however, add up to 75ml/2½fl oz/⅓ cup more gin to the mix before you pour it over the ice.

Blackcurrant cassis

Cassis is an intensely flavoured blackcurrant liqueur, and is generally used to add just a hint of colour and flavour to Champagne and sparkling wines. This home-made variation is so packed with the summer freshness of juicy blackcurrants that you'll want to ensure it is the predominant flavour in any cocktail.

Makes 6–8 glasses

225g/8oz/2 cups blackcurrants
50g/2oz/¼ cup caster (superfine) sugar
75ml/5 tbsp vodka
sparkling wine or Champagne

Cook's tip
For a less alcoholic version, either leave out the vodka from the syrup or top up the glasses with chilled sparkling mineral water instead of the wine or Champagne.

1 Using a fork, strip the blackcurrants from their stems. Scatter 50g/2oz/ ½ cup of the fruit into the sections of an ice-cube tray. Top up with cold water and freeze for about 2 hours.

2 Put the sugar in a small, heavy pan with 60ml/4 tbsp water and heat gently until the sugar has dissolved. Bring to the boil, remove from the heat, then pour into a jug and leave to cool. Push the remaining blackcurrants through a juicer and mix with the syrup. Stir in the vodka and chill until ready to serve.

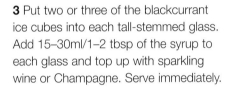

3 Put two or three of the blackcurrant ice cubes into each tall-stemmed glass. Add 15–30ml/1–2 tbsp of the syrup to each glass and top up with sparkling wine or Champagne. Serve immediately.

Mulled plums in marsala

You needn't confine mulled drinks to the festive season. This fruity version, distinctively spiced and laced with Marsala, is served chilled, so is perfect for drinks parties at any time of the year. This is a delicious and practical way of using an abundance of sweet, juicy plums to make an exotic drink that is guaranteed to impress your guests.

Makes 4 glasses

500g/1¼lb ripe plums
15g/½oz fresh root ginger, sliced
5ml/1 tsp whole cloves
25g/1oz/2 tbsp light muscovado
   (brown) sugar
200ml/7fl oz/scant 1 cup Marsala
ice cubes

3 Push the remaining plums through a juicer. Strain the syrup and mix with the plum juice and Marsala.

4 Put ice cubes and plum halves in four glasses and pour over the syrup. Serve with stirrers, if you like.

Cook's tip

If you are having a party, make a large batch of this drink. It can be transferred to a large punch bowl with a ladle so that your guests can help themselves and fish out the marsala-soaked plums.

1 Halve two of the plums and discard the stones (pits). Roughly chop the remainder. Put the ginger, cloves and sugar in a small pan with 300ml/½ pint/1¼ cups water. Heat gently until the sugar has dissolved then bring to the boil and add the halved plums.

2 Reduce the heat and simmer gently for 2–3 minutes until the plums have softened but still retain their shape. Using a slotted spoon, lift out the plums and leave the plums and syrup to cool.

Berried treasure

The combination of cranberries and raspberries is fast becoming a juice classic, despite the fact that these fruits are at their best during different seasons. This needn't hinder you though, just use one in frozen form – the fruit will thaw quickly and save you adding ice. This recipe uses raspberry conserve in place of the more usual sugar or honey to add sweetness.

1 Push all the raspberries through a juicer, followed by the raspberry conserve and then the cranberries.

2 Pour the juice into tall glasses, top up with soda water or sparkling mineral water and serve immediately.

Makes 2 tall glasses

250g/9oz/1½ cups raspberries
45ml/3 tbsp raspberry conserve
250g/9oz/1½ cups cranberries
soda water (club soda) or sparkling
   mineral water

Cook's tip

For a pretty presentation, thread a few of the berries on to wooden cocktail sticks (toothpicks) and rest them across the rim of the glasses. (To balance the sticks successfully, you'll need to use relatively narrow glasses.)

Mint julep

Traditionally, a julep is a sweetened, iced drink made using brandy or whisky and flavoured with fresh mint leaves. This stunning version infuses the mint in sugar syrup to colour it a cooling shade of green. Zipped up with brandy, or delicious peach brandy, and poured over ice, this makes a refreshingly good summertime tipple.

Makes 4 small glasses

25g/1oz/2 tbsp caster (superfine) sugar
25g/1oz fresh mint, plus extra mint sprigs, to decorate
crushed ice
100ml/7 tbsp brandy or peach brandy

Cook's tip
This sexy little number would be well placed in any cosmopolitan New York cocktail bar. To bring a little bit of that New York ambience into your home, prepare a large batch and invite plenty of friends round to help you drink it.

1 Put the sugar in a small, heavy pan with 200ml/7fl oz/scant 1 cup water. Heat gently until the sugar dissolves, then bring to the boil and boil for 1 minute to make a syrup. Pour into a small bowl. Pull the mint leaves from the stalks and add to the hot syrup. Leave the syrup to stand for about 30 minutes or until cool.

2 Strain the syrup into a blender or food processor, add the mint and blend lightly until it is finely chopped.

3 Half-fill four small glasses with crushed ice, packing one or two mint sprigs into each glass. Mix the brandy with the mint syrup and pour over the ice. Serve immediately.

Lime mojito

Cuba and the Caribbean islands have invented some of the most delicious lime- and rum-based cocktails, from tangily refreshing shorts to thick, creamy concoctions that are almost a meal in themselves. This recipes fits the first category, but beware, you're bound to find it irresistibly moreish – which could prove dangerous.

Makes 4 glasses

4 lemon balm sprigs
40ml/8 tsp caster (superfine) sugar
4 limes
130ml/4½fl oz/generous ½ cup white rum
ice cubes
strips of pared lime rind, to decorate
sparkling mineral water, to serve

Cook's tip
To ensure you get the maximum juice from the limes, microwave them for approximately 20–30 seconds on medium (50 per cent power).

1 Pull the lemon balm leaves from their stems. Put 10ml/2 tsp of the sugar into each small glass.

3 Squeeze the limes using a citrus juicer, or by hand, and then pour the juice into the glasses with the rum.

2 Add several lemon balm leaves to each glass and lightly rub the leaves into the sugar, using the back of a teaspoon, to release their fragrance.

4 Add plenty of ice to each glass and decorate with pared lime rind. Serve immediately, topped up with sparkling mineral water.

Tropical fruit royale

This recipe is a fresh and fruity variation of a kir royale, in which Champagne is poured over crème de cassis. Made with tropical fruits and sparkling wine, this cocktail is a lot less expensive than the Champagne version but still has a wonderfully elegant feel. Remember to blend the fruits ahead of time to give the mango ice cubes time to freeze.

Makes 6 glasses

2 large mangoes
6 passion fruit
sparkling wine

Cook's tip
Delight your guests with this delicious thirst-quencher. With its taste of the tropics, it makes the perfect choice for garden parties on balmy summer evenings, wherever in the world you are.

1 Peel the mangoes, cut the flesh off the stone (pit), then put the flesh in a blender or food processor. Process until smooth, scraping the mixture down from the side of the bowl, if necessary.

2 Fill an ice-cube tray with half of the purée and freeze for 2 hours.

3 Cut six wedges from one or two of the passion fruit and scoop the pulp from the rest of the passion fruit into the remaining mango purée. Process until well blended.

4 Spoon the mixture into six stemmed glasses. Divide the mango ice cubes among the glasses, top up with sparkling wine and add the passion fruit wedges. Serve with stirrers, if you like.

Pineapple and coconut rum crush

This thick and slushy tropical cooler is unbelievably rich thanks to the combination of coconut milk and thick cream. The addition of sweet, juicy and slightly tart pineapple, and finely crushed ice, offers a refreshing foil, making it all too easy to sip your way through several glasses.

1 Trim off the ends from the pineapple, then cut off the skin. Cut away the core and chop the flesh. Put the chopped flesh in a blender or food processor with the lemon juice and whizz until very smooth.

2 Add the coconut milk, cream, rum and 30ml/2 tbsp of the sugar. Blend until thoroughly combined, then taste and add more sugar if necessary. Pack the ice into glasses and pour the drink over. Serve immediately.

Makes 4–5 large glasses

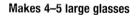

1 pineapple
30ml/2 tbsp lemon juice
200ml/7fl oz/scant 1 cup coconut milk
150ml/¼ pint/⅔ cup double (heavy) cream
200ml/7fl oz/scant 1 cup white rum
30–60ml/2–4 tbsp caster (superfine) sugar
500g/1¼lb finely crushed ice

Cook's tip
This is a great cocktail for making ahead of time. Blend the drink in advance and chill in a jug (pitcher). Store the crushed ice in the freezer ready for serving as soon as it's required.

Foaming citrus eggnog

For most of us, eggnog is inextricably associated with the festive season. This version, however, pepped up with orange rind and juice for a lighter, fresher taste, has a much wider appeal. Whether you sip it as a late-night soother, serve it as a wintry dessert or enjoy it as a cosy tipple on a wet afternoon, it's sure to bring a warm, rosy glow to your cheeks.

Makes 2 glasses

2 small oranges
150ml/¼ pint/⅔ cup single (light) cream
plenty of freshly grated nutmeg
2.5ml/½ tsp ground cinnamon
2.5ml/½ tsp cornflour (cornstarch)
2 eggs, separated
30ml/2 tbsp light muscovado (brown) sugar
45ml/3 tbsp brandy
extra nutmeg, for sprinkling (optional)

1 Finely grate the rind from the oranges, then squeeze out the juice and pour it into a jug (pitcher).

2 Put the rind in a small heavy pan with the cream, nutmeg, cinnamon and cornflour. Heat gently over a low heat, stirring frequently until bubbling.

3 Whisk the egg yolks with the sugar, using a handheld whisk.

4 Stir the hot citrus cream mixture into the egg yolks, then return to the pan. Pour in the orange juice and brandy and heat very gently, stirring until slightly thickened.

5 Whisk the egg whites in a large, clean bowl until foamy and light.

6 Strain the cream mixture through a sieve into the whisked whites. Stir gently and pour into heatproof punch cups, handled glasses or mugs. Sprinkle over a little extra nutmeg before serving, if you like.

Cook's tip
Note that this recipe contains almost raw egg.

Amaretto apricot dream

This really is a dream of a drink, combining fresh, ripe apricots, oranges and delicious maple syrup with creamy cool yogurt. Light and fruity, it is a wonderful choice for a breezy, sunny day in the garden, and the addition of almond liqueur and amaretti biscuits gives it a wonderfully complex flavour. Once you've tasted one you'll surely be back for more.

Makes 4 glasses

3 large oranges
600g/1lb 6oz small fresh apricots
60ml/4 tbsp maple syrup, plus extra
   to serve
50g/2oz amaretti
200g/7oz/scant 1 cup Greek (strained
   plain) yogurt
30ml/2 tbsp amaretto liqueur
mineral water (optional)
ice cubes

1 Grate the rind from one of the oranges and squeeze the juice from all three. Halve and stone (pit) the apricots and put them in a pan. Add the orange juice and zest then heat slowly. Cover with a lid and simmer very gently for 3 minutes or until the apricots are tender. Strain through a sieve, reserving the juice, and leave to cool completely.

2 Put half the fruit, the strained juice, maple syrup and amaretti in a food processor or blender and blend until smooth. Arrange the remaining fruit halves in the bases of four glasses.

3 Stir the yogurt until smooth and spoon half over the fruits. Add the amaretto, and a little mineral water to the blended mixture (if the juice is too thick), and pour into the glasses. Add the remaining yogurt and one or two ice cubes to each glass. Drizzle with maple syrup to serve.

Cook's tip

To impress guests at parties, use two teaspoons to delicately place a spoonful of yogurt on top of this apricot drink.

perfect
party
drinks

If you're entertaining a large crowd, whizzing up a
choice of interesting party brews is a sure-fire way
to get the occasion off to a lively start. From long
and refreshing spritzers to short, punchy tipples,
this chapter offers a feast of innovative choices
that include a couple of fresh fruit blends for
partygoers who prefer not to drink alcohol.

Lemon vodka

Very similar to the deliciously moreish Italian liqueur, Limoncello, this lemon vodka should be drunk in small quantities due to its hefty alcoholic punch. Blend the sugar, lemons and vodka and keep in a bottle in the refrigerator, ready for pouring over crushed ice or topping up with soda or sparkling water. It is also delicious drizzled over melting vanilla ice cream.

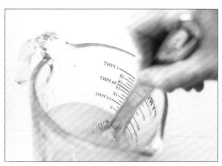

1 Squeeze the lemons using a citrus juicer. Pour the juice into a jug (pitcher), add the sugar and whisk well until all the sugar has dissolved.

2 Strain the sweetened lemon juice into a clean bottle or narrow-necked jar and add the vodka. Shake the mixture well to combine, and chill for up to 2 weeks.

3 To serve, fill small glasses with ice and pour the lemon vodka over.

Makes 12–15 small glasses

10 large lemons
275g/10oz/generous 1¼ cups caster
    (superfine) sugar
250ml/8fl oz/1 cup vodka
ice cubes

Cook's tip
Pure, clear vodka and zesty lemon juice make a tantalizing spirit that tastes like bottled sunshine. If you like, bruise a couple of mint leaves and add to the glass before pouring the vodka – this will add a delicious freshness to the drink.

Apple-tice

Even the dullest of eating apples seem to juice well. With the addition of a fresh mint syrup and sparkling cider, any apple juice can be transformed into a distinctly exciting, mildly alcoholic blend that makes an excellent party drink. The recipe allows you to choose how much cider you add to each glass, which makes it easier to control your alcohol consumption.

Makes 6–8 glasses

25g/1oz/1 cup mint leaves, plus extra mint
   sprigs, to decorate
15g/½oz/1 tbsp caster (superfine) sugar
6 eating apples
ice cubes
1 litre/1¾ pints/4 cups dry (hard) cider

4 To serve, add ice cubes and mint sprigs and top up with cider.

Cook's tip
If you'd prefer a non-alcoholic version of this drink, top up the glasses with sparkling mineral water, ginger ale or lemonade instead of cider.

1 Using a pair of kitchen scissors, roughly snip the mint into a heatproof jug (pitcher). Add the sugar to the jug, then pour over 200ml/7fl oz/scant 1 cup of boiling water. Stir well until the sugar has dissolved, then leave to stand until cool.

2 Drain the mint from the syrup and discard the mint leaves. Using a small, sharp knife, core the apples, chop them into chunks of roughly the same size and push them through a juicer.

3 Mix the apple juice and mint-flavoured syrup in a large jug and chill (preferably overnight, but for at least 1–2 hours) until ready to serve.

Cranberry and apple spritzer

Don't forget to look after the non-drinkers at your party – all too often they're left with just the mixers, fizzy drinks or tap water. This colourful, zingy cooler combines tangy cranberries with fresh juicy apples and a subtle, fragrant hint of vanilla. Topped up with sparkling mineral water, this is one spritzer that's sure to keep everyone happy.

Makes 6–8 glasses

6 red eating apples
375g/13oz/3½ cups fresh or frozen
cranberries, plus extra to decorate
45ml/3 tbsp vanilla syrup
ice cubes
sparkling mineral water

Cook's tip
To make vanilla syrup, heat a vanilla pod (bean) with sugar and water in a pan until the sugar dissolves. Simmer for 5 minutes then leave to cool.

1 Quarter and core the apples then cut the flesh into pieces small enough to fit through a juicer. Push the cranberries and apple chunks through the juicer. Add the vanilla syrup to the juice and chill until ready to serve.

2 Pour the juice into glasses and add one or two ice cubes to each. Top up with sparkling mineral water and decorate with extra cranberries, threaded on to cocktail sticks (toothpicks). Serve immediately.

Pink perfection

Make plenty of freshly juiced blends like this gorgeous combination and your guests will keep coming back for more. Raspberry and grapefruit juice make a great partnership, particularly if you add a little cinnamon syrup to counteract any tartness in the fruit.

Makes 8 tall glasses

1 cinnamon stick
50g/2oz/¼ cup caster (superfine) sugar
4 pink grapefruits
250g/9oz/1½ cups fresh or frozen raspberries
wedge of watermelon
crushed ice
borage flowers, to decorate (optional)

Cook's tip
Make non-alcoholic drinks more interesting by dressing them up with extra fruits and decorations. As an alternative to watermelon, serve other stirrers such as cinnamon sticks, or provide sugar stirrers so guests can sweeten their drinks to suit their own personal preference.

1 Put the cinnamon stick in a small pan with the sugar and 200ml/7fl oz/scant 1 cup water. Heat gently until the sugar has dissolved, then bring to the boil and boil for 1 minute. Reserve to cool.

2 Cut away the skins from the pink grapefruits. Cut the flesh into pieces small enough to fit through a juicer funnel. Juice the grapefruits and raspberries and pour into a small glass jug (pitcher).

3 Remove the cinnamon from the syrup and add the syrup to the grapefruit and raspberry juice in the jug.

4 Carefully slice the watermelon into long thin wedges and place in eight tall glasses. Half-fill the glasses with the crushed ice and sprinkle with borage flowers, if you like. Pour over the pink fruit juice and serve immediately with plenty of napkins to allow your guests to eat the watermelon wedges.

Cherry berry mull

Inspired by the traditional warm spices used to flavour mulled wine, this sweet and fruity punch makes a novel drink for barbecues and summer parties. Nothing brings out the irresistible flavours of soft summer fruits quite like juicing, and the orange liqueur and spices add both a wonderfully rounded taste and a feisty kick to the drink.

2 Push the strawberries, raspberries, cherries and redcurrants alternately through a juicer and pour the juice into a large jug (pitcher).

3 Strain the cooled syrup through a sieve into the fruit juice, then stir in the liqueur. Serve in small glasses, decorated with cherries and redcurrants, and serve with cinnamon stirrers, if you like.

Cook's tips

To make an outrageous decoration, tie a couple of cherry stalks to a stem of redcurrants and balance these dramatically on the edge of each cocktail glass to really impress your guests.

Warm spices and cool soft fruits go surprisingly well together. This unusual, refreshing drink is just perfect for al fresco drinking and, believe it or not, is equally good without the alcohol.

Makes 8 small glasses

2 cinnamon sticks, halved
15ml/1 tbsp whole cloves
15g/½oz/1 tbsp golden caster (superfine) sugar
300g/11oz/2¾ cups strawberries
150g/5oz/scant 1 cup raspberries
200g/7oz/scant 1 cup pitted cherries, plus extra to decorate
150g/5oz/1¼ cups redcurrants, plus extra to decorate
60ml/4 tbsp Cointreau or other orange-flavoured liqueur
extra cinnamon sticks for stirrers (optional)

1 Put the cinnamon sticks in a small pan with the cloves, sugar and 150ml/ ¼ pint/⅔ cup water. Heat gently until the sugar dissolves, then bring to the boil. Remove from heat and leave to cool.

Cuba libra

Rum and coke takes on a much livelier, citrus flavour with this vibrant Caribbean cocktail that's sure to put you in the mood to party. The wonderful flavour and aroma of freshly squeezed limes is the dominant taste in this blend, and the dark rum really packs a punch when combined with the sweet, syrupy cola drink.

Makes 8 glasses

9 limes
ice cubes
250ml/8fl oz/1 cup dark rum
800ml/1⅓ pints/3½ cups cola drink

Cook's tip
If you run short of limes during your party, add some freshly squeezed lemon juice instead.

1 Thinly slice one lime then, using a citrus juicer, squeeze the juice from the rest of the limes. Put plenty of ice cubes into a large glass jug (pitcher), tucking the lime slices around them.

2 Add the lime juice to the jug, then the rum and stir with a long-handled spoon. Top up with cola drink and serve in tall glasses with stirrers.

Peach bellini

Serve this classic, fabulous cocktail when peaches are at their most delicious and best. Preserved stem ginger and peach juice ice cubes make an unusual twist, so allow plenty of time for them to freeze before serving. If using both brandy and sparkling wine is a little too alcoholic for your taste, top up the cocktail with sparkling mineral water instead of the wine, or alternatively omit the brandy. In fact, any combination would be equally delicious.

Makes 8–10 glasses

75g/3oz preserved stem ginger (about 5 pieces), sliced
6 large ripe peaches
150ml/¼ pint/⅔ cup peach brandy or regular brandy
1 bottle sparkling wine

Cook's tip

When the ice cubes start to melt you will get an extra hit of peach and ginger juice in your drink. Drink this cocktail slowly to allow all of the flavours to merge.

1 Place one or two slices of ginger in all the sections of an ice-cube tray. Halve and stone (pit) the peaches then push through a juicer. Make 200ml/7fl oz/ scant 1 cup of the peach juice up to 300ml/½ pint/1¼ cups with water. Pour into the ice-cube tray. Freeze.

2 When frozen solid, carefully remove the ice cubes from the tray and divide among eight to ten wine glasses. Stir the brandy into the remaining peach juice, mix well and pour over the ice cubes. Top up with the sparkling wine and serve immediately.

Tropical storm

Whisky and ginger makes a popular flavour combination in party drinks and cocktails, either served neat or blended with other ingredients to dilute the intense flavour. This incredibly refreshing creation with mango and lime has, not surprisingly, plenty of kick.

Makes 8 tall glasses

2 large ripe mangoes
2 papayas
2 limes
150ml/¼ pint/⅔ cup ginger wine
105ml/7 tbsp whisky or Drambuie
ice cubes
lime slices and mango and papaya wedges, to decorate
soda water (club soda)

Cook's tip

Mango and papaya sometimes collects inside the juicer rather than flowing easily into the container. If this happens, pour a little cold water through the juicer funnel.

1 Halve the mangoes either side of the flat stone (pit). Using a spoon, scoop out the flesh from the halves and cut from around the stone using a small, sharp knife. Chop roughly.

2 Halve the papaya and discard the pips (seeds). Remove the skin and roughly chop the flesh. Cut away the skins from the limes and halve.

3 Push the mangoes, papayas and limes through a juicer. Pour into a jug (pitcher), add the ginger wine and whisky or Drambuie and chill until ready to serve.

4 Place plenty of ice cubes and long wedges of mango and papaya and slices of lime into tall glasses. Pour over the juice until the glasses are two-thirds full. Top up with soda water and serve.

Happy days

Set a midsummer drinks party off to a good start with this fabulously fruity blend. It's packed with summer fruits and flavoured with refreshingly light, but highly intoxicating, Limoncello – a welcome alternative to the more traditional spirits used in party blends.

1 Using a fork, strip the redcurrants from their stalks. Reserve 50g/2oz/ ½ cup. Hull the strawberries and reserve 200g/7oz/1¾ cups. Push the remainder through a juicer with the redcurrants. Pour into a glass punch bowl or jug (pitcher) and stir in the liqueur. Chill until ready to serve.

2 Halve the reserved strawberries and add to the juice with the redcurrants, plenty of ice cubes and the mint or lemon balm. Top up with lemonade or cream soda, and serve.

Makes 8 glasses

250g/9oz/generous 2 cups redcurrants
675g/1½lb/6 cups strawberries
200ml/7fl oz/scant 1 cup Limoncello liqueur
ice cubes
small handful of mint or lemon balm
I litre/1¾ pints/4 cups lemonade or
   cream soda

Cook's tip

Limoncello is an intensely tangy, very alcoholic Italian lemon liqueur. It's great served on its own over plenty of crushed ice or, more unusually, in this fruity punch. If you can't find it, use a well-flavoured orange liqueur such as Cointreau or Grand Marnier instead.

Grand marnier, papaya and passion fruit punch

The term "punch" comes from the Hindi word *panch* (five), relating to the five ingredients traditionally contained in the drink – alcohol, lemon or lime, tea, sugar and water. The ingredients may have altered somewhat over the years but the best punches still combine a mixture of spirits, flavourings and an innocent top-up of fizz or juice.

Makes about 15 glasses

2 large papayas
4 passion fruit
300g/11oz lychees, peeled and pitted
300ml/½ pint/1¼ cups freshly squeezed
  orange juice
200ml/7fl oz/scant 1 cup Grand Marnier or
  other orange-flavoured liqueur
8 whole star anise
2 small oranges
ice cubes
1.5 litres/2½ pints/6¼ cups soda water
  (club soda)

1 Halve the papayas and discard the seeds. Halve the passion fruit and press the pulp through a sieve into a small punch bowl or a pretty serving bowl.

2 Push the papayas through a juicer, adding 100ml/7 tbsp water to help the pulp through. Juice the lychees. Add the juices to the bowl with the orange juice, liqueur and star anise. Thinly slice the oranges and add to the bowl. Chill for at least 1 hour or until ready to serve.

3 Add plenty of ice cubes to the bowl and top up with soda water. Ladle into punch cups or small glasses to serve.

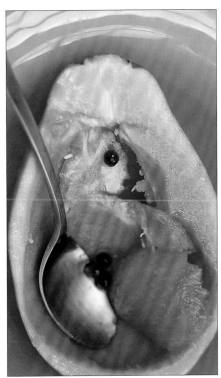

Apple-spiced beer

Lager takes on a whole new dimension in this fun and fruity cooler. Diluted with freshly squeezed apple juice and flavoured with ginger and star anise, it's a great drink for anyone who wants to pace themselves through a party. The spiced apple juice can be made several hours in advance and chilled in a serving jug, ready for topping up at the last minute.

Makes 8–10 tall glasses

8 eating apples
25g/1oz fresh root ginger
6 whole star anise
800ml/1⅓ pints/3½ cups lager
crushed ice

1 Quarter and core the apples and, using a small, sharp knife, cut the flesh into pieces small enough to fit through a juicer. Roughly chop the ginger. Push half the apples through the juicer, then juice the ginger and the remaining apples.

2 Put 105ml/7 tbsp of the juice in a small pan with the star anise and heat gently until almost boiling. Add to the remaining juice in a large jug (pitcher) and chill for at least 1 hour.

3 Add the lager to the juice and stir gently to help disperse the froth. Pour over crushed ice in tall glasses and serve immediately.

Cucumber pimm's punch

This tangy blend of freshly juiced cucumber, ginger and apples isn't as innocent as it looks – or tastes. It's lavishly topped with alcohol, so is definitely a drink to enjoy on a lazy summer afternoon. To enjoy on a picnic, just chill the juice really well, pour into a vacuum flask and top up with chilled ginger ale when you reach your destination.

2 Peel the remaining cucumber and cut it into large chunks. Roughly chop the ginger and apples. Push the apples, then the ginger and cucumber through a juicer and pour the juice into a large jug (pitcher) or bowl.

3 Stir the Pimm's into the juice, add the cucumber, lemon slices and mint and borage sprigs, then chill.

4 Just before serving, add the ice cubes and borage flowers to the punch and top up with ginger ale. Ladle into glasses or glass cups.

Makes 12 small glasses

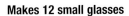

1 cucumber
1 lemon
50g/2oz fresh root ginger
4 eating apples
600ml/1 pint/2½ cups Pimm's
sprigs of mint and borage
ice cubes
borage flowers
1.5 litres/2½ pints/6¼ cups ginger ale

1 Cut off a 5cm/2in length from the cucumber and cut into thin slices. Slice the lemon and set both aside.

index